THE AKAN (TW

The Akan (Twi-Fante) Language

ITS SOUND SYSTEMS AND TONAL STRUCTURE

Florence Abena Dolphyne

WOELI PUBLISHING SERVICES
ACCRA
2006

Published by
Woeli Publishing Services
P. O. Box NT 601
Accra New Town
Ghana

Tel. 227182 / 229294
Fax. 229294 / 777098
Email. woeli@libr.ug.edu.gh

ISBN 9988 – 626 – 67 – 3

PRODUCED IN GHANA

Typesetting by the Author, Prof Florence A. Dolphyne
Printed by Black Mask Printing Press, Accra

To
KOFI
and
AKUBA

Acknowledgements

I wish to place on record my sincere gratitude to J. M. Stewart, formerly of the Institute of African Studies, University of Ghana, for the detailed comments and suggestions he made on an earlier draft of this book.

My thanks also go to other coleagues in the University of Ghana, in particular, M. E. Kropp Dakubu and A. S. Duthie for their comments on Chapter Three.

Some of the dialect differences were cross-checked with my students, and I am grateful to them for their co-operation. Special mention must be made of G. Menscer for his insight into the workings of the Asante dialect.

The maps were made by the staff of the cartographic section of the Geography Department of the University of Ghana. Earlier versions of this text were typed by H. L. Achuson. E. A. Annor helped in getting this material ready for photo-offset printing. To all of them I am most grateful.

The specimen Akan texts in Appendix II have been reproduced here with the kind permission of the Bureau of Ghana Languages.

The final version of this book was completed during my year at U.C.L.A. on a Fulbright grant, and I am grateful to the United States Council for International Exchange of Scholars for the grant which made this work possible, and to Professor P. Ladefoged, Head of the Phonetics Department, for making the facilities of the Department available to me.

Finally, my husband, Kofi, and my daughter, Akuba, deserve special mention for their patience and moral support throughout the period this material was being prepared.

CONTENTS

Acknowledgements   vii

Introduction   xi

Chapter 1   - The Vowels of Akan
- Introduction   1
- Phonetic Description of Vowels   5
- Distribution of Vowels   7
- Vowel Harmony   14

Chapter 2   - The Consonants of Akan
- Introduction   26
- Phonetic Description of Consonants   26
- Distribution of Consonants   31
- The Glottal Stop   48

Chapter 3   - Tone in Akan
- Introduction   52
- The Syllable in Akan   52
- The basic Tones   55
- Downdrift   56
- Downstepped High tone   59
- Gliding pitches   61
- Functions of tone   66
- Tone patterns of the major word classes   75

Chapter 4   - The Structure of Akan Words
- Introduction   79
- Nominal Affixes   82
- Adjectival Affixes   86
- Verbal Affixes   87
- The Structure of the Simple Stem   97
- The Tone of the Verb Stem   111

Chapter 5 - Compounds 117
  - Introduction 117
  - The Phonology of Compounds 117
  - Reduplicated forms 124

Chapter 6 - Sound Correspondences between Akuapem, Asante and Fante
  - Introduction 139
  - Some Phonological Processes in Akan 139
  - Summary of Dialect Differences 151

Chapter 7 - The Unified Akan Orthography
  - Introduction 154
  - Representation of Vowel Harmony 154
  - Representation of Tense / Aspect Affixes 156
  - Pronouns and Pronominal prefixes 158
  - Asante Nominal Suffixes 159
  - Vowel Alternation in Verbs 160
  - Rounding of Vowels 160
  - Representation of certain consonants 161
  - Representation of CVC(V) Stems 163
  - Miscellaneous 166

Select Bibliography on Akan Phonology 168

Appendix I - The Verbal Paradigm
  - Non-Ingressive forms 172
  - Ingressive forms 184

Appendix II - Specimen Passages in the Unified Akan Orthography 191

MAPS 1 & 2 195

Subject Index 197

INTRODUCTION

The Akan Language

The name Akan has, since the 1950's, been used in Ghana to refer to the language whose dialects include Fante, Akuapem, Asante, Bron, Wasa, Agona, Akyem, Kwahu, etc. (see Map 1). These dialects are spoken in the Brong-Ahafo, Ashanti and Central Regions, and in parts of the Western and Eastern Regions of Ghana by about 40% (1960 Census) of Ghana's12.2 million people (1984 Census) as a first language. Akan is also spoken as a second language by the Anyi (Aowin), Sehwi, Nzema and Ahanta to the West, and by speakers of Guan languages such as Efutu/Awutu and Anum-Kyerepong-Larteh to the South and East (Map 1). In these areas, (except in the Nzema-speaking area) Akan is the medium of instruction in the first few years of Primary School, and it is used in Church and for trade. Akan is also an important language of trade in the Ga-speaking state capital, Accra.

Three Akan dialects, Akuapem, Fante and Asante, have achieved literary status. Each has a written form which reflects the peculiarities of the particular dialect, so that it is not easy for an Asante speaker who does not speak Fante to read a text written in Fante, and vice-versa, even though the two dialects are mutually intelligible. The obvious disadvantages of this situation, such as the cost of producing the same text in three different orthographies, each with a limited readership, led to a demand in the 1950's for a single written form which would be acceptable to the speakers of all three dialects. It was during this period that the name Akan was adopted as the name of the language whose written dialects are Akuapem, Fante and Asante. This was an important step, for until that time the overall language as such did not have a name. Twi was generally used to refer to the Akuapem and Asante dialects, and people spoke of Twi and Fante as if they were different languages. Indeed there were separate radio programmes in Twi and in Fante.

The name Akan is also used to refer to the people who live in most of the coastal and forest areas of Ghana and the Ivory Coast. These people share a common culture, which distinguishes them from other ethnic groups in West Africa. They speak languages/dialects which include Baule, Anyi (Aowin), Sehwi (Sanvi), Nzema, Ahanta, Fante, Akuapem, Asante, Brong, Wasa, etc. (see Map 2). These languages/dialects are all closely related, and have a large number of vocabulary in common. Together they constitute a language family that Stewart named the Tano language family because they extend to the east and west of the Tano river.

The Akan people are therefore a very large ethnic group living in Ghana and in the Ivory Coast, who speak languages and dialects that are classified under the Tano language family, to which the Akan language belongs. In order to distinguish between the two uses of the name Akan, this book is entitled the Akan (Twi-Fante) language.

Why a book on Akan phonology

The Akan Orthography Committee, which was set up in1952 to work out a unified orthography for the Akan language, took a decision, in 1978, on the form the unified Akanorthography should take. Most of the decisions were based on the relationships between the sound systems of the three written dialects, hence the need for a book explaining what these relationships are, so that users of the unified Akan orthography can understand the basis for the new Akan spelling. Moreover, since the introduction of Akan as a Sixth Form G.C.E. 'Advaned' Level subject, it has been felt by many Akan scholars that at the Sixth Form level, the distinction made at the G.C.E. 'Ordinary' Level, where students do either Akuapem Twi, Asante Twi or Fante, should be dropped, and that Sixth Form students should be encouraged to study the Akan language, and learn about the differences between the dialects. The differences between Akuapem, Fante and Asante exist more in the sound systems than in the grammar. Some of these differences have been discussed in papers published in academic journals, but these papers are written in a way that only a specialist in Linguistics can understand. This book is an attempt to present in one volume, a comprehensive discussion of the differences between these three dialects, and every effort has been made to keep technical terminology to a minimum.

In 1970 Parliament decided that as far as possible every Ghanaian school child should be taught a second Ghanaian language in addition to his/her own mother tongue. This led to the establishment of the School of Ghana Languages in Ajumako, where specialist teachers of Ghanaian languages are trained. The student teachers learn a second Ghanaian language in addition to their own. This book is primarily meant as a textbook for the students of Akan at the School of Ghana Languages.

Undergraduate students of Linguistics, both Ghanaian and non-Ghanaian, will also find the book a useful introduction to the phonology of this major language of Ghana.

CHAPTER 1

THE VOWELS OF AKAN

I   INTRODUCTION

A   Oral Vowels

The vowel sounds of Akan are represented in the orthography by seven vowel letters:

$$i \quad e \quad \varepsilon \quad a \quad \mathtt{o} \quad o \quad u$$

Each of the vowel letters **e** and **o** stands for two vowel sounds.

e : i) a fairly high vowel quality as in

tẹw   'to tear'   kɛsẹ   'big'

ii) a lower vowel quality as in

fie   'house'   esiw/esie   'anthill'

o : i) a fairly high vowel qualiy as in

tọw   'to throw'   họrọ   'to wash'

ii) a lower vowel quality as in

obi   'somebody'   ako   'parrot'

As will be explained in the section on Vowel Harmony, the higher vowel qualities **ẹ** and **ọ** occur in the same word with the vowels **ɛ** and **ɔ**, while the lower qualities **e** and **o** occur with the vowels **i** and **u**. It is thus generally possible to predict which quality is required in any given word. The symbols **ẹ ọ** for the higher vowel qualities will be used only when such a prediction is not possible. Akan therefore has nine distinct vowels.

$$i \quad \mathring{e} \quad e \quad \varepsilon \quad a \quad \mathtt{o} \quad o \quad \mathring{o} \quad u$$

1

The vowels occur in the following words

siw	'plug a hole'
sɛw	'sharpen'
gye	'receive' (Akuapem)
sɛw	'spread out'
saw	'dance'
sɔw	'catch'
dwo	'cool down' (Akuapem)
sọw	'bear fruit'
suw	'be worn out/ decay'

In the Akuapem and Asante dialects there is a tenth vowel quality, which may be symbolised as **ạ**, which occurs mainly before syllables with the vowels **i** and **u**, as in the following words:

dạạbi	'no'	pạtu	'pretend'
kạri	'weigh'	mạtu /mạạtu	'I've dug it up'

This vowel is a variant of the **a** vowel when it occurs before syllables with the vowels **i** and **u**. It also occurs before **o** in the words

ạko	'parrot'	ạgoo	'knocking!'

The Fante dialect has the vowel **e** in this position, as shown in the words below.

deebi	'no'	petu	'pretend'
ker	'weigh'	eko	'parrot'

There are some sub-dialects of Fante however (e.g. Bɔrbɔr Fante) in which this vowel occurs, and it occurs *after* syllables with the vowels **i**, **u**.

bisạ	'ask'	osua	'it is small'

2

a̜ will be represented throughout this text with **a**.

In Asante, **ɛ** and **e** replace **a** when **a** occurs as the final vowel of a word that is followed by the Progressive form of the verb, as shown below in square brackets. (In Asante the Progressive form of the verb is realised as a lengthening of the preceding vowel.)

Asante:	Ama reba	[Amɛɛba]	'Ama is coming'
	Ama redidi	[Ameedidi]	'Ama is eating'
compare			
	Kofi reba	[Kofiiba]	'Kofi is coming'

Throughout this text, whenever it becomes necessary to indicate the pronunciation of a word or sentence, the pronunciation will be enclosed in square brackets, as in the above examples.

In Fante **ɛ** and **e** replace **a** when **a** occurs as the final vowel of a word that is followed by an Imperative form, as shown below.

| Fante: | ma nkɔ | [mɛ nkɔ] | 'don't go' |
| | ma ndzi | [me ndzi] | 'don't eat it' |

Throughout this text, where it is necessary to indicate different pronunciations that occur in particular dialects, the dialects will be indicated as follows:

(Ak) for Akuapem; (As) for Asante; (Fa) for Fante.

B Nasalised Vowels

The vowels discussed so far are oral vowels. In addition to these, there are five nasalised vowels:

$$ ī \quad ē̞ \quad ā \quad ọ̄ \quad ū $$

During the production of these vowels some of the air comes out through the nose. Vowel nasality is not indicated in Akan orthography, although it is phonemic, that is, it can bring about a difference in the meanings of words that are otherwise identical. In the following examples nasality of vowels is indicated by ¯ above the vowel letter.

3

fī̃	'dirt'	fi	'go out'
sẽ	'teeth'	sẹ / sẹw	'sharpen'
kā̃	'say'	ka	'be left behind'
tọ̄	'bake'	tọ / tọw	'throw'
hū̃	'see'	hu / huw	'blow air'

Oral and nasalised vowels contrast after voiceless consonants, as in the above examples. Nasalised vowels do not occur before or after semivowels in Akan, hence the vowels that occur before **w** in the above examples are all oral. Nasalised vowels occur after nasal consonants in stem words, but they do not occur after non-nasal voiced consonants such as **b, d,** unless the vowel is followed by a nasal consonant. (See Chapter 4 for a more detailed discussion.) This text will, in the main, follow Akan orthography in not indicating vowel nasality except where, as in the above examples, special attention is being drawn to nasalised vowels.

The vowel qualities **o ɛ ɔ o** are not normally nasalised in Akan. However **ɛ** and **ɔ** are nasalised in Fante before the nasal consonants **m** and **n.**

fɛ̃m	'borrow / lend'	tɔ̃n	'sell'
bɛ̃n	'be near'	kɔ̃m	'hunger'

ɛ, ɔ are oral before **m**, and only slightly nasalised before **n** in Asante.

fɛm	'borrtow / lend'		kɔm	'hunger'
bɛn	[bɛny]	'be near'	tɔn	[tɔŋw]	'sell'

(see CVn(V) stems in Chapter 4)

In Akuapem, **ɛ** and **ɔ** are oral in such words. However, nasalised **ɛ̃** occurs in a few words in Akuapem.

	kɛ̃	'by all means' (probably borrowed from Gã)		
	hĩɛ̃	'open'	tɛ̃ɛ̃	'straighten'
compare Asante:	hīnī̃	'open'	tɛ̃nɛ̃	'straighten'

The vowel **o** is nasalised in the Fante word **muo** 'to be bad'

4

pronounced [mõ]. It is only in this word that a nasalised [õ] is known to occur in Akan.

C   Long Vowels

All Akan vowels can be either long or short, and a difference in vowel length alone can bring about a difference in meaning.

| da | 'day' | daa | 'everyday' |
| kɔ | 'go' | kɔɔ | 'red' |

Long vowels are usually represented by two vowel letters.

II   PHONETIC DESCRIPTION OF VOWELS

Vowel sounds are generally described in terms of the shape of the tongue and the lips when the vowel is being made.

A   Part of tongue, that is, the part of the tongue that is closest to the roof of the mouth when the vowel is being made. Three types of vowels are distinguished in this way:

ɛ   as in hwɛ 'look at' is a **front** vowel, that is, made with the
front part of the tongue.
a   as in da 'sleep' is a **central** vowel, that is, made with the
central part of the tongue.
ɔ   as in tɔ 'buy' is a **back** vowel, that is, made with the back part
of the tongue.

B   Height of tongue, that is, the relative height of the tongue in the mouth, in relation to the palate, when the vowel is being made. Four types of vowels are distinguished in this way:

i   and u as in mihu 'I see it' are **close** vowels

e   and o as in ose 'jubilation' are **half-close** vowels

ɛ   and ɔ as in ɔhwɛ 'he looks at' are **half-open** vowels

a   as in da   'sleep' is an **open** vowel

These vowels are also sometimes re-grouped into three types.

i is a **high** vowel

e and ε are **mid** vowels

a is a **low** vowel

C **Lip position,** that is, the shape of the lips when the vowels are being made. Akan vowels show a distinction between two types of vowels, rounded and unrounded vowels.

u as in bu 'break' and

ɔ as in tɔ 'buy' are **rounded** vowels

They are vowels during the production of which the corners of the lips are brought forward.

i as in fi 'go out' and

a as in da 'sleep' are **unrounded** vowels.

They are vowels for which the lips do not assume the position described above.

D **Oral/Nasal,** that is, whether, all the air involved in the production of the vowels comes out through the mouth, in which case they are referred to as **oral** vowels, or whether the air comes out through both the mouth and the nose, in which case they are referred to as **nasalised** vowels. Nasalised vowels are normally represented with ⁓ over the vowel letter.

| fi | 'go out' | fĩ | 'dirt' |
| ka | 'be left behind' | kã | 'say' |

The vowel diagram that follows indicates the approximate tongue positions for the vowel sounds of Akan.

Note : [a̤] has been put in square brackets on the vowel chart because it does not normally occur in a word by itself as the other vowels do. It is a variant of **a** that occurs mainly before i and u. It has a quality that range

6

from a front vowel quality close to ɛ in the Asante dialect, to a more central quality in the Fante subdialects in which it occurs.

Vowel Chart

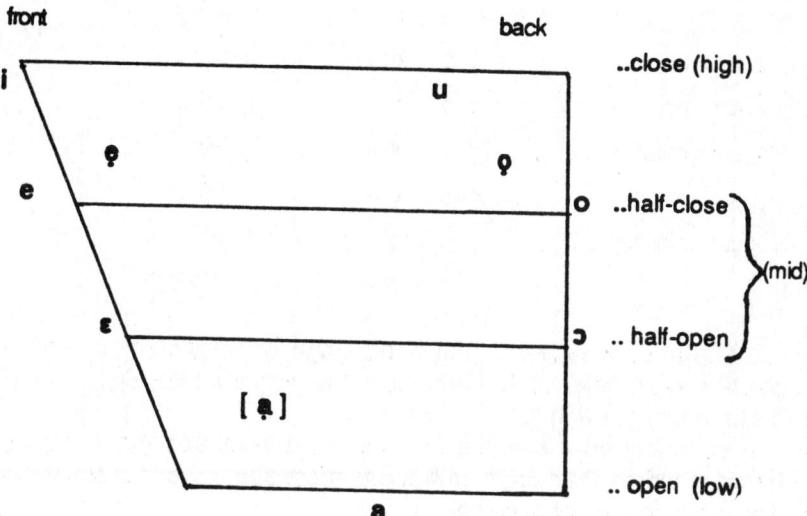

The following generalised statements can be made about Akan vowels.

1. All **back** vowels in Akan, **u ọ o ɔ**, are **rounded.**
2. All **front** vowels **i ẹ e ɛ** and the **central** vowel **a** are **unrounded**
3. **High** and **low** vowels in Akan have **oral** and **nasalised** counterparts

    i ɪ ẹ ẽ a ã ọ õ u ũ

4. **Mid** vowels in Akan are **oral**: e ɛ ɔ o

III DISTRIBUTION OF VOWELS

A Word-Initial vowels

Not all of the different vowels can occur in word-initial position, that is, at the beginning of words. The following examples show the word-initial vowels that occur in the different dialects.

	Akuapem, Asante		Fante		
e	eti / etire	i	itsir	'head'
ɛ	ɛnam	ẹ	ẹnam	'meat/fish '
		or ɛ	ɛnam	'meat/fish'
a̧	ani	e	enyiwa	'eyes'
a	aba	a	aba	'seed'
o	ohia	i	ihia	'poverty'
		or o	ohia	'poverty'
ɔ	ɔhẹnẹ	ẹ	ẹhẹn	'chief/king'
		or ɔ	ɔhẹn	'chief/king'

Mid and low vowels, that is non-high vowels, occur in word-initial position in all dialects. In Fante only, the high front vowels, i and ẹ also occur in this position.

In Asante only, e and ɛ occur in word-initial position in the citation forms of words that begin with a nasal consonant, and also when such words occur in emphatic speech.

ensuo	for	nsuo	'water'		ɛmpa	for	mpa	'bed'
endi	for	ndi	'don't eat it'		ɛŋkɔ	for	ŋkɔ	'don't go'

B   Vowel sequences within words

The chart that follows shows the vowel combinations that occur within individual words. Long vowels are considered in this analysis as a sequence of two identical vowels.

8

	i	ẹ	e	ɛ	a	ɔ	o	ọ	u
i	ii		ie	iɛ	ia		io		
ẹ		ẹẹ		ẹɛ	ẹa				
e	ei		ee						
ɛ		ɛẹ		ɛɛ					
a		aẹ			aa				
ɔ		ɔẹ				ɔɔ			
o	oi						oo		
ọ		ọẹ		ọɛ	ọa	ọɔ		ọọ	
u	ui		ue		ua		uo		uu

These vowel sequences occur in the following words:

ii	pii	'many'
ie	sie	'hide'
iɛ	abiɛsa	'three' (Ak)
ia	tia	'step on'
io	bio	'again'
ẹẹ	mee	'be full /eat enough'
ẹɛ	teɛ	'straighten ' (Ak)
ẹa	kyea	'be bent'
ei	seesei	'now'
ee	hwee	'empty'
ɛẹ	sɛe	'destroy'
ɛɛ	ɔhwɛɛ	'he looked at ...'
aẹ	kae	'remember'

aa	daa	'everyday'
ɔẹ	ɔkɔe	'he went'
ɔɔ	kɔɔ	'red'
oi	edwoi	'it cooled down' (Ak)
oo	apoo	'cheating'
ọẹ	ɔkoe	'he fought'
ọɛ	foɛ	'be feverish'
ọa	boa	'help'
ọɔ	ɛboɔ	'stone' (As)
ọọ	ɔtoo	'he baked ...'
ui	ohui	'he saw it'
ue	bue	'open/ uncover'
ua	bua	'cover'
uo	afuo	'farm ' (As)
uu	ohuu	'he saw ...'

The above vowel sequences occur
1. within stem words, and
2. at morpheme boundaries

1. Within stem words

sie	'hide'		tia	'step on '
nwiinwii	'grumble'		mẹẹ	'eat enough'
kaẹ	'remember'		sɛẹ	'destroy'
apoo	'cheating'		bua	' cover'

2. At morpheme boundaries:

i) in Past Tense forms of the verb (the stem is underlined)

(a) Past Tense forms with the suffix i / ẹ

odii 'he ate it'   ɔgyeẹ 'he received it' (As. Fa.)

10

ogyei	'he received it' (Ak)	ɔhwɛ̣ɛ̣	'he looked at it'
edwoi	'it cooled down'(Ak)	ɔtɔ̣ɛ̣	'he bought it'
ohui	'he saw it'	ɔtọẹ	'he baked it'
esiwii	'it got blocked'(Ak)	ɔkasaẹ	'he spoke'
onumii	'he sucked it'	ɔnọmẹẹ	'he drank it'

(b) Past Tense forms without the suffix i / ẹ

These are Past Tense forms that are immediately followed by an object or a complement. The verb stem must end in a vowel.

odii kosua	'he ate an egg'	ɔtɔɔ ntama	'he bought cloth'
ohuu nọ	'he saw him'	ɔbaa ha	'he came here'
ogyee nọ	'he received him' (Ak)	ɔkasaa pii	'he talked a lot'

ii) in Progressive forms of the verb in Asante, as indicated in square brackets below.

merekɔ	[mẹẹkɔ]	'I am going'
ɔredidi	[oodidi]	'he is eating'
yɛrefa	[yɛɛfa]	'we are taking it'

iii) in Perfect and Consecutive forms of the verb :

ɔadi	[waadi /weedzi]	'he has eaten it'(Ak.Fa.)
yɛafa	[yaafa]	'we've taken it' (Ak. Fa.)
moafa	[mọafa]	'you (plu.) have taken it'

iv) in Asante nouns with the suffix e / ɛ ; o / ɔ
   (this suffix does not occur in Akuapem and Fante)

As: esie	compare Ak. Fa: esiw		'anthill'
adẹɛ		adẹ /adzẹ	'thing'

11

As: owuo		Ak.Fa: owu	'death'
ɛbɔɔ		ɔbɔ	'stone'

v) at word boundaries in compounds

| aniasɛ | 'under the eyes' | anɔasɛm | 'boast/vain talk' |
| ahɔɔdɛn | 'strength' | ntɛasɛ(ɛ) | 'understanding' |

C   Vowel sequences between words

When a word that ends in a vowel is followed by another that begins with a vowel, the vowel sequences that occur are as follows:

1.   If the initial vowel of the *second* word is **e ɛ o ɔ** (in all dialects) or
ɛ i in Fante

a)   This vowel is dropped if the word occurs in a noun phrase in which it is in apposition to, or in possessive relationship with the preceding noun.

Kumasɛ hɛnɛ	not	Kumasɛ ɔhɛnɛ /ɛhɛn	'Kumasi chief'
dua nɔ sɔ	not	dua nɔ ɛsɔ	'the top of the tree'
Kofi dan	not	Kofi ɔdan / ɛdan	'Kofi's house'

Note : The deletion of the initial vowel of the second word occurs even when the first word ends in a consonant:

| Nkran hɛnɛ | not | Nkran ɔhɛnɛ / ɛhɛn | 'the chief of Accra' |

b)   In other phrases this initial vowel of the second word is not always deleted. In the following examples both sentences are acceptable, although the sentences to the right are the more normal. Those to the left will be used in rather deliberate speech.

fa ɛnam /ɛnam nɔ kɔ	or	fa nam nɔ kɔ
		'take the meat/fish away'
ɔatɔ ɔkraman ba	or	ɔatɔ kraman ba
		'he's bought a puppy'

tọ(w) ɛwura /iwura nọ gu	or	tọ(w) wura nọ gu
		'throw the rubbish away'
saa onipa yi	or	saa nipa yi
		'this person'

Again the optional deletion of the initial vowel of the second word applies even where the first word ends in a consonant.

kum oguan /iguan nọ	or	kum guan nọ
		'slaughter the sheep'

Note : Where the **o** or **ɔ** prefix of the second word is the third person singular pronoun prefix, it is never deleted.

mahu onua nọ	'I've seen his brother/sister' (As)
kɔfrɛ ɔnana bra	'go and call his grandparent' (As.)
nẹa obetumi na ɔdẹ bɛba	'he'll bring what he can'

2. If the initial vowel of the second word is **a** (all dialects) or **e** (Fa. only) this vowel is never deleted, whether the first word ends in a vowel or a consonant.

di aduanẹ nọ /dzi edziban nọ	'eat the food'
dua nọ asẹ	'under the tree'
ɔatɔn akongua/ egua nọ	'he has sold the chair'

3. In all dialects where, as in 1 (b) and 2 above, the vowel of the second word is pronounced, a final mid vowel **e ɛ o ɔ** or low vowel **a** of the *first* word is replaced by a vowel the same quality as the following vowel.

In Fante this is also true of any final high vowel, **i ẹ ọ u,** of the first word. If the final vowel of the first word is a back vowel, the preceding consonant is labialised, that is, pronounced with lip-rounding, as in the first two examples below.

ɔrẹkɔ aba	[ɔrẹkwaaba]	'he's going, but will be back'

13

eno ada	[ɛnwaada]	'mother is asleep' (As.)
hwɛ abɔfra nɔ	[hwaabɔfra nɔ]	'look at the child'
ɔba ɔhɛn(ɛ) hɔ	[ɔbɔɔhɛn(ɛ) hɔ]	'he comes to the chief'

Fante:

dzi edziban nɔ	[dzeedziban nɔ]	'eat the food'
ɔtsɛ asɛ	[ɔtsaasɛ]	'he understands'
wobotu ɔhɛn nɔ	[wobotɔɔhɛn nɔ]	'they'll destool the chief'
ɔasɔ awar	[waaswaawar]	'she's of age (to marry')

compare Ak. and As.

di aduanɛ nɔ	[di aduanɛ nɔ]	'eat the food'
ɔtɛ asɛ(ɛ)	[ɔtɛ asɛ(ɛ)]	'he understands'
wobetu ɔhɛnɛ nɔ	[wobetu ɔhɛnɛ nɔ]	'they'll destool the chief'
ɔasɔ awarɛ(ɛ)	[wa(a)sɔ awarɛ(ɛ)]	'she's of age'

In order to make reading sound natural, it is important that these restrictions on the type of vowel sequences that can occur between words in a sentence are observed.

IV VOWEL HARMONY

A The General Rules

1. Advanced tongue root harmony

The distribution of the nine (Fa.) or ten (Ak.As.) vowel qualities of Akan in words is such that it is possible to group the vowels into two sets as follows: (note: Fante does not have a̤)

| Set I | i | e | a̤ | o | u | (advanced vowels) |
| Set II | ɪ | ɛ | a | ɔ | o̤ | (unadvanced vowels) |

In general, in any Akan word of two or more syllables, only the vowels of one set may occur. This means that there is a restriction on the distri-

14

bution of these vowels which does not generally allow the vowels of Set I to occur in the same word with the vowels of Set II. The following examples illustrate this point.

Set I		Set II	
wubetu	'you'll dig it up'	wǫbɛtǫ(w)	'you'll throw'
odi	'he eats '	ɔdẹ	'he is called ..'
maadi/meedzi	'I've eaten it'	maatɔ	'I've bought it'
owu(o)	'death'	ɛwǫ(ɔ)	'honey'

For this reason verbal affixes have two different pronunciations depending on whether they occur with a verb stem that has Set I or Set II vowels. Some Fante verbal affixes have four different pronunciations. These are discussed later.

a) Subject-Concord prefixes (pronoun prefixes)

1st person singular	**mi**		**mẹ**	
	midi	'I eat'	mẹdẹ	'I am called..'
2nd person singular	**wu** / **I** (Fa)		**wǫ** / **ǫ** (Fa)	
	wudi /		wǫdẹ /	
	idzi	'you eat'	ẹdzẹ	'you're called..'
3rd person singular	**o**		**ɔ**	
	odi	'he eats'	ɔdẹ	'he is called..'
Impersonal (Ak, As.)	**e**		**ɛ**	
	edi	'it eats up'	ɛdẹ	'it is called..'
1st person plural	**ye**		**yɛ**	
	yedi	'we eat'	yɛdẹ	'we're called..'
2nd person plural	**mu**		**mǫ**	
	mudi	'you eat'	mǫdẹ	'you're called..'
3rd person plural	**wo**		**wɔ**	
	wodi	'they eat'	wɔdẹ	'they're called..'

b) Tense / Aspect affixes

Future prefix	**be**			**bɛ**	
	obehu	'he'll see'		ɔbɛkɔ	'he'll fight'
Past suffix	**i**			**e̩**	
	ohui	'he saw'		ɔko̩e̩	'he fought'
Perfect prefix	**a̩** / **e** (Fa.)			**a**	
	ɔahu / oehu	'he's seen'		ɔakɔ	'he has fought'
Ingressive prefixes	**be**			**bɛ**	
	obehu	'he comes and sees'		ɔbɛkɔ	'he comes and fights'
	ko			**kɔ**	
	okohu	'he goes and sees'		ɔkɔkɔ	'he goes and fights'

The restriction on the distribution of vowels which makes it necessary for the vowels of only one set to occur in any given word is referred to as Vowel Harmony. Vowel Harmony in Akan is a property of the word, that is, it characterises a whole word at a time.

The two different vowel qualities associated with each of the verbal affixes above make it possible for Akan vowels to be paired off as follows :

$$i / e̩, \quad e / ɛ, \quad a̩ / a, \quad o / ɔ, \quad o̩ / u$$

The vowels on the left in each pair are the Set I vowels and those to the right are the corresponding Set II vowels. A close study of the way in which these vowel sounds are made shows that in each pair of vowels, the Set I vowel is made a little further forward and higher in the mouth than the Set II vowel, that is, **i** as in midi 'I eat' is made a little further forward and higher in the mouth than **e̩** in me̩de̩ 'I am called..'; and **e** in obehu 'he will see it' is articulated further forward and higher in the mouth than **ɛ** in ɔbɛkɔ 'he will fight', and so on.

During the articulation of Set I vowels, **i e a̩ o u**, the base or root of the tongue is pushed forward, and this enlarges the space in the pharynx (the space in the throat above the larynx or voice box), hence the hollow quality that characterises these vowels. The vowel **a̩** does not have this hollow quality in Asante and Akuapem, and there is evidence (Lindau 1979) that in Asante, this vowel does not have the root of the tongue pushed forward during its articulation. However, in the Fante subdialects in which it occurs, **a̩** does have the hollow quality that characterises Set I vowels. (see note on page 7 for a description of the vowel qualities associated with **a̩** in the different dialects).

16

Set II vowels, ɛ̣ ɛ a ɔ ọ , are articulated with the base or root of the tongue pushed back or retracted, and this narrows the space in the pharynx during the articulation of these vowels. On account of this, the Set I vowels are referred to as having **advanced** tongue root, and the Set II vowels as having **unadvanced** or retracted tongue root position.

Akan therefore basically has five vowels units, each of which has two vowel qualities associated with it depending on whether it occurs in a word that has advanced vowels or a word that has unadvanced vowels. These five vowel units and the vowel qualities associated with them are as follows :

(1) i   a High Front vowel pronounced   i   or   ẹ

(2) e   a Mid Front vowel pronounced   e   or   ɛ

(3) a   a Low Central vowel pronounced   ạ   or   a

(4) o   a Mid Back vowel pronounced   o   or   ɔ

(5) u   a High Back vowel pronounced   u   or   ọ

The old Gold Coast script had five vowel letters, and distinguished between each pair of non-low advanced and unadvanced vowels by the presence or absence of a subscript dot. This system reflected the vowel harmony relationship between the vowels of the language, unlike the the current Akan orthography which confuses the issue by using the letters e and c to represent two sounds each, one of which is advanced and the other unadvanced. Moreover each advanced / unadvanced vowel associated with these vowel letters belongs to a different pair of advanced/ unadvanced vowels. For example, the letter e represents two vowel qualities, the advanced e vowel which pairs off with ɛ and the unadvanced ẹ which pairs off with i.

In the table that follows, the system used in this text is put in brackets where it is different from present-day Akan orthography.

The Gold Coast script did not distinguish between advanced and unadvanced a.

	Gold Coast script	Present-day Akan orthography
advanced	ị	i
vowels	ẹ	e
	a	a (ạ)
	ọ	o
	ụ	u

17

unadvanced	i		e	(ẹ)
vowels	e		ɛ	
	a		a	
	o		ɔ	
	u		o	(ọ)

The Akan vowel system therefore has five basic vowel units, each of which has two different pronunciations associated with it depending on whether it occurs in a word that is characterised as advanced or unadvanced, as in the following examples.

efie	'home'	**ɛfẹ(ɛ)**	'vomit'
owu(o)	'death'	**ɛwọ(ɔ)**	'honey'
adi	'outside'	**adẹ(ɛ)**	'thing'

2.   Rounding Harmony

In addition to having two sets of verbal prefixes depending on whether the vowel of the verb stem is advanced or unadvanced, Fante verbs have an additional feature of vowel harmony in which only vowels that are rounded or only vowels that are unrounded can occur in certain verbal prefixes, depending on whether the verb stem has rounded or unrounded vowels. Such verbal affixes have four different pronunciations associated with them, as illustrated by the following examples.   The prefixes are **me**, the 1st person singular pronominal prefix, pronounced [mu mọ mi mẹ]; **re,** the Progressive prefix pronounced [ru rọ ri rẹ]; and **kɔ**, the 'going' Ingressive prefix pronounced [kọ kɔ ke kɛ].

murukotu	'I'm going to dig it up'	**mọrọkɔtọw**	'I'm going to throw it'
mirikedzi	'I'm going to eat it'	**mẹrɛkɛtsẹw**	'I'm going to pluck it'

This type of vowel harmony, the rounding or unrounding of the vowels in affixes and stems, occurs in the first person singular pronoun prefix and in all Tense / Aspect prefixes, except the Perfect, in Fante verbal forms.   It also occurs in Fante 1st and 3rd person possessive pronouns.   In Asante, the nominal suffixes **e/ɛ , o/ɔ** agree in lip

18

position with the vowel of the noun stem.

Fa:	mu̷ nu kun	'my/her husband'	mo̷ no̜ kɔn	'my/his neck'
	mi̷ni tsir	'my/his head'	me̜/ne̜ kyɛw	'my/his hat'
As:	owuo	'death'	ɛwo̜ɔ	'honey'
	esie	'anthill'	ase̜ɛ	'the base of'

Labial or rounding/unrounding vowel harmony also occurs in the reduplicated forms of some verbs in which the vowel of the prefix has the lip position of the vowel of the stem, even though the vowel quality may be different. (Reduplication is a type of compound formation in which the stem or part of the stem is repeated.)

dwo	: dwudwo	'cool down' (Ak)	tɔn	: to̜ntɔn	'sell'
gye	: gyigye	'receive' (Ak.)	hwɛ	: hwe̜hwɛ	'look for'
tu	: tutu	'dig up'	to̜	: to̜to̜	'bake'

All these examples of vowel harmony involve partial assimilation of the vowels of the affixes, in other words the vowels in the affixes take on one feature - tongue root position -, or two features - tongue root and lip positions -, of the stem. Some speakers of Cape Coast Fante (Abaka,1978) have complete assimilation in prefixes of Progressive verbs when the stem is a reduplicated monosyllabic form with an advanced high vowel. As can be seen from the following examples, the three prefixes, me̜, the 1st person singular pronoun prefix; re̜, the Progressive prefix; and kɔ and bɛ, the Ingressive prefixes, have the same vowel quality as that of the verb stem. Only the vowel of the first part of the reduplicated form is pronounced in these verbs.

mirikedzidzi	[miri /miikiidzi]	'I'm going to eat'
miribedzidzi	[miri /miibiidzi]	'I'm about to eat'
murukotutu	[murukuutu]	'I'm going to dig up'

B Exeptions to Vowel Harmony

There are a few exceptions to the rules of Vowel Harmony described above, that is, there are words in which both advanced and unadvanced vowels occur, and these are as follows :

1. In stem words unadvanced vowels follow advanced vowels. The central vowel **a** is the unadvanced vowel that usually occurs in such words, although **ɛ** also occurs in the two words below.

bisa	'ask'	pinkyɛ	'come close' (Fa.)
kura	'hold'	nyinsɛn	'be pregnant'
dua	'tree'	ohia	'poverty'

Such 'mixed' stems have two harmony spans: they have advanced vowels in prefixes, in harmony with the first syllable of the stem, and unadvanced vowels in suffixes, in harmony with the second syllable of the stem.

yekobisaẹ	'we went and asked'	onyinsɛnẹẹ	'she became pregnant'
obekuraẹ	'he came and held it'	wohyiaẹ	'they met'

compare stems with single harmony spans :

obẹpusuwii	'he came and shook it'	ɔbɛkyẹrɛẹ	'he came and pointed it out'

2. Syllables with the open central vowel **a** after

    i) a palatal or palatalised consonant such as **gy, tw, si [sy]**
    ii) certain labialised consonants represented in the orthography as
           su, gu, hu,
take only advanced vowels in preceding syllables. Vowels occurring after the **a** vowel are unadvanced, so that such words have two harmony spans, advanced - unadvanced.

(i)	Onyamẹ	'God'	obegyaẹ	'he came & left it'
	misianẹẹ	'I descended'	obedwanẹ	'he will run away' (As)
	yekotwa	'we go and cut it'	ohwaẹ	'he begged for food' (As)
(ii)	esua	'it is small'	obeguan	'he will run away'
	obehuaẹ	'he came and begged for food'	oguarẹẹ	'he had a bath'

20

As far as these exceptions to the vowel harmony rule are concerned, Stewart (1966 b) noted that Koelle's 'Polyglotta Africana', which has a list of Akan words recorded in the 19th Century, has the form gia for present-day gya indicating that the Akan speakers he recorded at that time pronounced the word as gia. In other words present-day gya was a 'mixed' stem like those discussed in (a) above. Over the years the **g** consonant was influenced by the following high front vowel **i** and became a palatal consonant, but the effect of the advanced **i** vowel on preceding syllables remained, hence the two harmony spans associated with this stem and the other palatal and palatalised consonants in (i) above.

The labialised consonants represented as **su**, **hu** are articulated with the back of the tongue raised and pushed forward in the position for the vowel **u**. This is also true of the consonant represented as **gu**, in which **g** has a much further forward articulation on the palate than the first consonant in ɔkwan 'road', for example. It is considered here that these consonants are articulated with advanced tongue root position, and this is why only advanced vowels occur in syllables that precede them.

Note : (a) The palatal consonant **ky** and the labialised consonants **kw**, **ŋw** are not affected by this rule, and vowels occurring in preceding syllables are unadvanced, like **a**.

ákyakya	'hunchback'	ɔkwan	'road'
ɔbɛnwansi	'he'll sneeze'		
kwaw	'polish floor'	kɔkwaw	(reduplicated form,
compare			unadvanced vowel in prefix)
gua	'split open'	gugua	(reduplicated form,
			advanced vowel in prefix)
gya(w)	'leave behind'	obegya(w)	'he will leave behind'

(b) When the palatal consonants occur before other vowels, the normal rules of vowel harmony apply.

obetwi	'he'll push it'	ɔbɛtwɛ	'he'll pull it'
yegyinaɛ	'we stopped'	yɛgyeɛ	'we received it'(As. Fa)

3. In the Akuapem dialect the Progressive prefix **rɛ** is always pronounced with an unadvanced vowel quality whether the verb stem has

21

advanced or unadvanced vowels. Vowels preceding this prefix are also unadvanced, so that where the verb stem is advanced, the Progressive form has two harmony spans.

ɔrɛdidi	'he's eating'	ɔrɛfa	'he's taking it'
ɔrɛkodidi	'he's going to eat'	ɔrɛkɔfa	'he's going to take it'

compare

As: ookodidi	'he's going to eat'	ɔɔkɔfa	'he's taking it'
Fa: orikedzidzi	'he's going to eat'	ɔrɛkɛfa	'he's going to take it'

4. Although the a vowel as in mạdi 'I've eaten it' is advanced, only unadvanced vowels occur in syllables that precede it. Since this vowel occurs mainly before syllables with i or u such words have two harmony spans, unadvanced - advanced.

ɔpạtui	'he pretended'	mọakạri	'you (pl.) have weighed it'
wɔbɛkạri	'they will weigh it'		

The noun ɔbạrima 'man' has three harmony spans, unadvanced-advanced-unadvanced, because advanced a takes an unadvanced prefix ɔ before it, and the stem is a mixed advanced - unadvanced stem.

Like other advanced vowels, a occurs before syllables that have any of the palatal or labialised consonants referred to in (c) above followed by a.

ạgya	'father'	ạgua	'chair' (Ak.)
mạtwa	'I've cut it'	ạhua	'one who begs for food'

5. Suffixes that begin with a consonant, such as

-fọ(ɔ), -nọm, -yɛ, -ni

do not harmonise with the vowels of the stem. The vowels in the suffix remain advanced or unadvanced, as the case may be.

Abibifọ(ɔ)	'Africans'	kununọm	'husbands'

ohuuyɛ   'he saw it'(As.)   Lateni   'a citizen of Larteh'

In Lateni above, the unadvanced vowel ɛ in Latɛ 'Larteh town' is replaced with the corresponding advanced vowel, e in Lateni. This is becaucse ɛ occurs before the advanced vowel i in the suffix ni. (See vowel harmony between words, Section C, below.)

6.   In Asante only, where a stem ends in an advanced mid vowel, that is, e or o, this vowel is replaced by its unadvanced equivalent, ɛ or ɔ, respectively, before the Past suffix and the -i/-ҽ nominalising suffix.

wie	:	owiɛɛҽ /owiɛɛyɛ	'he finished it'
suro	:	osurɔɔҽ /osurɔɔyɛ	'he was afraid'
hwire	:	ehwirɛɛҽ /ehwirɛɛyɛ	'it got pierced'
wie	:	awiɛyɛ	'the end'
sie	:	asiɛyɛ	'cemetery'

This is the only instance where an advanced vowel is replaced by its unadvanced equivalent. Compare Akuapem and Fante forms :

wie	:	owiei, awiei	suro	:	osuroi
sie	:	osiei, asiei	hwire	:	ehwirei

C   Vowel Harmony between words

1.   The general rule ⸝

Vowel harmony rules apply between words in sentences and in compounds where a word with unadvanced vowels e.g. ɔkɔ 'he goes' is followed by a word with advanced vowels e.g. fie 'home'. The unadvanced vowel immediately preceding the advanced vowel is replaced by the corresponding advanced vowel, hence

[ɔko fie]   'he goes home'

This process of replacing an unadvanced by an advanced vowel does not normally extend beyond the syllable immediately preceding the advanced vowel, as in the example above. For some speakers however,

23

the vowels in the other syllables may also be replaced by the corresponding advanced vowel. as in [oko fie]. The process is called assimilation, and it takes place when, as in the example above, one sound ɔ is replaced by another sound o under the influence of a third sound i which is near to it in the word or sentence. In each of the following examples the unadvanced vowel becomes advanced under the influence of a following advanced vowel.

(i) Compounds :

bɔ	and	din	:	[abodin /abodzin]	'praise/ title'
asɛm	and	hunu	:	[asenhunu]	'useless talk'
ɔhẹnẹ	and	fie	:	[ahimfie]	'palace'

(ii) Sentences :

	ɔpɛ sika	:	[ɔpe sika]	'he likes money'
	mɛkɔ Kumasẹ	:	[mɛko Kumasẹ]	'I'll go to Kumasi'
	frɛ Kofi	:	[fre Kofi]	'call Kofi'
but	din and sɛẹ	:	[dinsɛẹ]	'slander'
	Kofi kɔ	:	[Kofi kɔ]	'Kofi has gone'

There is no assimilation in the last two examples because the unadvanced vowel *follows* the advanced vowel in each case.

Across word boundaries, unadvanced high vowels, ẹ and ọ, are often not fully assimilated to an advanced i or u quality when they occur before words with advanced vowels. They take on a quality that is between ẹ and i, ọ and u respectively. For some speakers the vowels remain unadvanced in this position, as in the following examples.

ahẹmfie	not	ahimfie	'palace'
ɔtẹ Kumasẹ	not	ɔti Kumasẹ	'he lives in Kumasi'
ɔatọ Kusi	not	ɔatu Kusi	'he's caught up with Kusi'

Note: Between words in compounds and in sentences ạ or e is the advanced vowel that corresponds to unadvanced a in Akuapem and Asante, as illustrated by the following examples. in Fante it is always e.

24

Compounds			Stem(s)	
bisebisa	(reduplicated form)	:	bisa	'ask'
gyinągyina / gyinegyina (redup.)		:	gyina	'stand'
dwenini	'ram'	:	odwaŋ, nin	'sheep','male'

Sentences

brą mu	come in'	:	bra, mu	'come','inside'
bre fie	'come home'	:	bra, fie	'come','home'

Vowel harmony in these examples is basically a process of regressive or anticipatory assimilation, that is, the unadvanced vowel that is assimilated precedes the advanced vowel that assimilates.

2. Exception

The rule of regressive assimilation between words does not apply when the unadvanced vowel occurs before an advanced vowel which is itself an assimilated vowel.

kɔtɔ bɛdi	pronounced	kɔtɔ bedi	'go buy it and eat it'
sɔrę kɔtwa	pronounced	sɔrę kotwa	'get up, go and cut it'

CHAPTER 2

THE CONSONANTS OF AKAN

INTRODUCTION

The thirty four consonants of Akan are represented in the orthography by sixteen letters of the alphabet. Some letters like n and w
stand for more than one consonant, such as n in nam 'walk' and kan
'read' (Ak.), and w in ɔwɔ 'snake' and wie 'finish'. However, as will be
explained under distribution of consonants, it is possible to tell from the
context which consonant sound is required.

Some other consonants are represented by two letters, such as the
initial consonants in gye 'receive', and hwie 'pour out'.

The consonants are shown on the consonant chart in the next
section.

II PHONETIC DESCRIPTION OF CONSONANTS

Consonants are generally described in terms of the following:

- A) place of articulation
- B) manner of articulation
- C) presence or absence of voicing
- D) secondary articulation

A   Place of articulation

Nine consonant types are distinguished in Akan according to the
place of articulation, that is, the points in the mouth where the sound is
made.

i)   **Bilabial**: sounds made with the two lips, e.g. **p, b, m**

ii)   **Labio-dental**: sounds made with the lower lip and the upper
teeth e.g. **f**

iii) **Alveolar**: sounds made with the tip of the tongue and the
alveolar or teeth ridge (the part of the gum immediately behind the upper
front teeth) e.g. **t, d, n**

iv) **Pre-palatal** (alveolo-palatal) : sounds made with the front part
of the tongue and the area behind the alveolar ridge, while the middle

26

part of the tongue is raised e.g. **ky** as in kyɛw 'hat'

v) **Palatal**: sounds made with the middle part of the tongue and the hard palate e.g. **ny** as in Onyame̩ 'God'

vi) **Labial-palatal**: sounds made with the middle part of the tongue raised towards the hard palate while the lips are brought together. The labial-palatal sound in Akan involves a rounding of the lips, **w** as in owia 'sun'

vii) **Velar**: sounds made with the back of the tongue raised towards the soft palate (velum) e.g. **k, g**

viii) **Labial-velar**: sounds made with the back of the tongue raised towards the velum while the lips are brought together. The labial-velar sound in Akan involves a rounding of the lips, **w** as in ɔwɔ 'snake'

ix) **Glottal**: sounds made in the glottis, i.e. inside the larynx or voice box e.g. **h** as in ɛhɔ 'there'.

B   Manner of articulation

Seven types of consonants are distinguished in Akan according to the manner of articulation, that is the way in which air from the lungs is modified at the place of articulation.

i)   **Plosive** : sounds made when air from the lungs is first completely blocked at some point in the mouth and then released suddenly so that air escapes from the mouth with a slight explosive sound e.g. **p, t, d, k**

ii)   **Affricate** : sounds made when air is first completely blocked as for a plosive sound, and then released slowly e.g. **ky** as in kyɛw 'hat'

iii)   **Nasal** : sounds made when the air is completely blocked in the mouth, but the passage through the nose is open so that all the air comes out through the nose e.g. **m, n**

iv)   **Lateral** : sounds made when air escapes along the sides of the tongue e.g. **l** as in lɔɔre 'lorry'

v)   **Trill** : sounds made when the tip of the tongue makes several quick contacts with the area behind the teeth ridge. eg. **r** as pronounced by some Akuapem speakers.

vi)   **Fricative** : sounds made when air escapes through a narrow passage in the mouth so that friction is heard e.g. **f, s, hy**

vii) **Approximant** (frictionless continuant and semivowel): sounds made when air escapes through a relatively wide passage so that there is no friction e.g. **r, w**. Semivowels (Glides) are so called because they are vowel articulations which are so short that they are not heard as vowels, for example **y** in yɛ 'do' is a short **i**, and **w** in ɔwɔ 'snake' is a short **u**.

27

C   Presence or absence of voicing

Two types of consonants are distinguished according to whether or not the vocal cords (or vocal folds), which are located in the larynx or voice box, are vibrating when the sound is being made. When the vocal cords are vibrating they produce a buzzing sound. The vibration of the vocal cords may be felt by placing a finger on the voice box (Adam's apple) while making the sound **m** . For a sound like **f** no such vibration can be felt.

The two types of consonants are :

i)   **Voiced** consonants : consonants made when the vocal cords vibrate e.g. **b**, **m**, **r**

ii)   **Voiceless** consonants : consonants made when the vocal cords do not vibrate e.g. **p**, **s**, **ky**.

D   Secondary articulation

Consonants may be modified during their articulation, and this is referred to as secondary articulation. In Akan consonants may be modified in three ways. They may be

i)   **Labialised**, that is, with the lips rounded while the sound is being made. Labialisation involves a marked protrusion of the lips, and is represented by **w** after the consonant that is labialised e.g. **kw** in ɔkwan 'road'

ii)   **Palatalised**, that is, with the body of the tongue raised towards the hard palate when the consonant is being made e.g. Fante pronunciation of pɛ as [pyɛ] 'to like' or ben as [byẽn] 'to be well cooked'.

iii)   **Labial-palatalised**, that is, with the body of the tongue raised towards the hard palate while the lips are rounded when the consonant is being made e.g. dua 'tree' pronounced [dɥia]. There is no protrusion of the lips during labial-palatalisation. The lip-rounding is the type that occurs in the consonant in owia 'sun'. In Akan this is represented in the orthography by the letter **u** after the consonant, followed by a low or a mid vowel letter, as in dua 'tree', bue 'open' (As.).

The Consonant Chart that follows shows the classification of Akan consonants according to Place and Manner of Articulation. An attempt has been made to indicate the phonetic representation of some of the sounds, and these have been put in square brackets.

28

Consonant Chart

	Bilabial	Labio-dental	Alveolar	Pre-palatal/ Palatal	Velar	Glottal
Plosive	p b		t d		k kw g gu	
Affricate			ts (Fa) dz	ky [tɕ] gy [dʑ] tw [tɕɥ] dw [dʑɥ]		
Nasal	m		n	ny [ɲ] nw [ɲɥ]	n [ŋ] nw [ŋw]	
Lateral			l			
Trill			r (Ak)			
Fricative		f	s si [sy] su	hy [ɕ] hw [ɕɥ]		h hu
Approximant/ Glide	w w [ɥ]		r	y ([ɥ])	(w)	

From the consonant chart the following generalised statements may be made about the consonants of Akan.

a) Only plosives and affricates have voiced and voiceless counterparts.

b) Akan fricative sounds are voiceless.

c) The nasals, the lateral, the trill and the approximants are voiced.

d) Palatal (including alveolo-palatal), velar and glottal consonants have labialised and non-labialised counterparts e.g. **hy : hw**; **k : kw**.

29

The consonants occur in the following words:

p	pam	'sew'	apem	'thousand'
b	bu	'break'	aban	'government'
t	tɔ	'buy'	ntɛm	'quickly'
d	di	'eat'	ade(ɛ)	'thing'
k	ko	'fight'	ɔkɔm	'hunger'
g	ɡ-ʌ	'be soft'	agor(u/ɔ)	'recreation'
kw	kwaw	'polish floor'	ɔkwan	'road'
gu	guare	'have a bath'	oguan	'sheep'
ts	tsew	'pluck' (Fa)	itsir	'head' (Fa.)
dz	dzi	'eat' (Fa)	adze	'thing' (Fa.)
ky	kyɛ	'share out'	ɔkyena	'tomorrow'
gy	gye /gye	'receive'	ogya	'fire'
tw	twe	'pull'	etwa	'scar'
dw	dwiriw	'pull down'	adwen(e)	'brain'
l	lɔɔre	'lorry'	akɔlaa	'child' (As.)
m	me	'I'	mpam	'don't sew it'
n	nantew	'walk'	kan	'read' (Fa.)
ny	nyin	'grow'	Onyame	'God'
nw	enwin	'shade'	nwiinwii	'grumble'
n [ŋ]	ngo	'palm oil'	nkwan [ŋkwaŋ]	'soup' (Ak)
nw [ŋw]	aṅwa	'cooking oil' (As.)	nwansi	'sneeze'
f	fa	'take'	efie	'home'
s	sew	'sharpen'	asɔ	'hoe'
hy	hyɛ	'wear'	ɔhyew	'heat'
hw	hwie	'pour out'	ahwerew	'sugarcane'
h	hu	'see'	ɛhɔ	'there'
hu	huam	'nice smell'	ahua	'one who begs for food'
w	ware	'marry'	tew	'pluck'

30

w [ɥ]	wie	'finish'	owia	'sun'
r	reba	'is coming'	sɔre/sɔr	'get up'
y	yi	'remove'	ɔyare	'illness'

III DISTRIBUTION OF CONSONANTS

i) All Akan consonants can occur in word-initial position, but only the following consonants can occur in word-final position: **m** (all dialects), **n** (Fa.), **ŋ** (Ak.), **w** (Ak. Fa.), **r** (Fa.).

ii) The consonants **r** and **ŋ** do not occur in stem-initial position. In other words, there are no verb stems, nouns or adjectives that begin with **r** or **ŋ**. **ŋ** occurs only as a prefix in word-initial position in words like ŋkwaŋ 'soup' ŋkɔ 'don't go'. The name Araba, the Fante name for a girl born on Tuesday, is the only word in which **r** is known to occur in stem-initial position.

What follows is a detailed statement of the distribution of each of the consonants of Akan. Where no specific statement is made about the occurrence of a consonant before vowels, it means that consonant occurs before all vowels.

Plosives

1. **p** as in **pam** 'sew'.
This is a voiceless bilabial plosive.

p may be labialised, as in the word pue 'go out' pronounced   pwei in Fante. It may also be labial-palatalised, as in the Asante pronunciation of pue 'go out' as pɥie. Both types of labialisation are represented in the orthography with **u** after the consonant letter.

In Fante **p** is palatalised before front vowels.

| pii | 'many' | pronounced [pyii] |
| pɛ | 'like' | pronounced [pyɛ] |

2. **b** as in **bu** 'break'
This is a voiced bilabial plosive.

b may be labialised, as in the Fante pronunciation of bue 'open' as bwei.

A labial-palatalised **b** occurs in Asante.

bue [bɥie] 'open'   bua [bɥia]   'cover'

In Fante **b** is palatalised before front vowels.

ben [byẽn] 'be well cooked'   bɛn [byɛ̃n]   'be near'

In Akuapem and Asante, **b** is replaced by **m** when it is preceded by a nasal in the same word.

mbu   'not break' pronounced   mmu

mba   'children' pronounced   mma

3. **t** as in tɔ 'buy'
This is a voiceless alveolar plosive. A labial-palatalised **t** occurs in

tua [tɥia] 'pay for'   toa [tɥẽã] 'accuse/report on'(Fa)

In Fante **t** occurs only before back vowels and the central vowel **a**. Before front vowels, **ts** replaces **t**, as illustrated by the following examples where Akuapem and Asante **t** corresponds to Fante **ts**:

| Ak. As: tew | 'pluck' | Fa : tsew |
| eti(re) | 'head' | itsir |

This means that in Fante, **ts** is only a variant of **t** before front vowels, and they are therefore different pronunciations of the same basic consonant, that is, they are members of the same phoneme.

4. **d** as in da 'sleep'

This is a voiced alveolar plosive. A labial-palatalised **d** occurs in

dua [dɥia] 'tree'   aduan(e) [adɥiaŋ/ adɥianẽ] 'food'

In Fante **d** occurs only before back vowels and the central vowel, **a**. Before front vowels **dz** replaces **d**, so that as shown by the following examples, Akuapem and Asante **d** corresponds to Fante **dz** before front vowels.

dzi	'eat'		adze	'thing'

Like **t** and **ts**, **d** and **dz** are members of the same phoneme, that is, different pronunciations of the same basic consonant.

In Akuapem and Asante **d** is replaced by **n** when it is preceded by a nasal in the same word.

nda	'days'	pronounced	nna
ndi	'not eat'	pronounced	nni

5. **k** as in **ko** 'fight'.

This is a voiceless velar plosive. In all dialects **k** occurs before back vowels and the central vowel **a**. It occurs before front vowels in a few words such as

kɛse	'big'		okisi	'rat'
kɛtɛ	'mat'		ketewa	'small'

where the syllable in which **k** occurs is followed by one which begins with **s** or **t**. It also occurs before the high front vowel **e** in reduplicated forms.

kekaw	'bite'		kenkan	'read'

k is replaced by the affricate **ky** before front vowels in stem words.

kyi	'dislike'	kye	'catch'	kyɛ	'share out'

On the whole **k** and **ky** complement each other in their distribution, and like **t** and **ts** in Fante, **k** and **ky** are different pronunciations of the same basic consonant. It is worth noting that some older Akan speakers say ɔkɛna for ɔkyɛna 'tomorrow'.

k is labial-palatalised in Asante pronunciation of words like

Akua	[akɥia]	'name of a girl born on Wednesday'
okuafo	[okɥiafɔ]	'farmer'

6. **g** as in go(w) 'be soft'
This is a voiced velar plosive.
In Asante and Fante **g** occurs before the back vowels **u ɔ o** in a

few words. In Akuapem it only occurs before the advanced back vowels **u** and **o**.

gu	'be spread out'	agoo	'knocking!'
gɔ(w)	'be soft' (As.Fa.)	gow	'be soft' (Ak.)
agɔr(ɔ)	'recreation' (Fa.As)	agoru	'recreation' (Ak.)

It does not occur before front vowels. It occurs before the central vowel **a** in the following words.

gam	'grab/clutch at'
gagaga	an ideophone that refers to the noise made by the chattering of teeth or the cutting of bones.

Before front vowels **g** is replaced by **gy**, and like **k** and **ky**, **g** and **gy** complement each other in their distribution, and are considered different pronunciations of the same basic consonant, even though both of them occur before **a** in a few words.

In Akuapem **g** is replaced by **ŋ** when it is preceded by a nasal in the same word.

> ngow   'not soft'   pronounced   ŋŋow

7. **kw** as in ɔkwan 'road'.
This a labialised voiceless velar plosive.
kw occurs only before the central vowel **a**, so that it has very limited distribution. (See **tw** below.) In Fante it occurs before **e**, as in Kwesida 'Sunday', where this corresponds to Akuapem and Asante ạ.

8. **gu** as in gua 'market' (Ak., Fa.).
This is a labialised voiced velar plosive, but as explained earlier, (page 21) this consonant is articulated with an advanced tongue root position, so that it has a further forward articulation than **kw**. **gu** occurs in Akuapem and Fante before **a**. In Asante the corresponding sound is **dw** as illustrated by the following examples.

Ak. Fa. gua	'market'	As.	edwa
guan	'run'		dwane

In Akuapem and Fante **dw** mainly occurs before front vowels, and before back vowels in a few words. **gu** occurs only before **a**, so that **gu** and **dw** complement each other in their distribution in these two dialects. Although **dw** occurs before **a** in the following Akuapem words :

dwae   'haughtiness'   dwata   'cut up / divide'

it can be said that on the whole **gu** is replaced by **dw** before front and back vowels, and that **gu** and **dw** are different pronunciations of the same basic consonant.

Affricates

9.   **ts** as in itsir 'head' (Fante).
    This is a voiceless alveolar affricate.
    ts occurs only in Fante, and only before front vowels.

itsir   'head'   tsew   'pluck'

Before **ɛ** some Fante speakers have **ts**, while others have **t** .

ntsɛm/ntɛm   'quickly'

As stated earlier under **t**, **ts** replaces **t** before front vowels, and they are members of the same phoneme.

10.   **dz** as in dzi 'eat' (Fante)
    This is a voiced alveolar affricate.
dz occurs in Fante only, and before front vowels only.

dzi   'eat'   adze   'thing'

Before **ɛ** some Fante speakers have **dz** and others have **d**.

dzɛw/ dɛw   'burst into flames'

As stated earlier under **d**, **dz** replaces **d** before front vowels, and they are thus members of the same phoneme.

11.   **ky** as in kye(w) 'fry'.
    This is a voiceless pre-palatal (alveolo-palatal) affricate.
    ky occurs mainly before front vowels.

kyi   'dislike'   kyɛ(w)   'hat'

As stated earlier under **k**, **k** and **ky** complement each other in their distribution, and are considered different pronunciations of the same basic consonant.

ky occurs before **a** in the following words only:

akyakya   'hunchback'   kyawkyaw   'a type of sandals'

12. **gy** as in gye 'receive'.

This is a voiced pre-palatal (alveolo-palatal) affricate.

gy occurs before front vowels and **a**, as in

gyina 'stand'   **gye**   'receive'   gya(w)   'leave behind'

As explained earlier under **g**, **gy** and **g** complement each other in their distribution, and are members of the same phoneme.

In Akuapem and Asante **gy** is replaced by **ny** when it is preceded by a nasal.

ngyina   'not stand'   pronounced   nnyina

ngye   'not receive'   pronounced   nnye

13. **tw** as in twa 'cut'

This is a labialised voiceless pre-palatal affricate. The place of articulation for this consonant is further forward on the palate than it is for **ky**. Lip-rounding for **tw** is of the type referred to as labial -palatalisation and represented by the symbol **ɥ**

tw occurs mainly before front vowels and **a**, as in

twe   'pull'   **twɛn**   'wait'   **twa**   'cut'

It also occurs before back vowels in a few words, like the following:

ntwoma   'red clay'   ntwo   'defeat' (Ak)

twuw/ twiw   'push' (Ak.Fa.)

Although **tw** contrasts with **kw** before a, (that is, both occur before

36

a), since velar and palatal consonants in Akan generally complement each other in their distribution in so far as velar consonants do not occur before front vowels but palatal consonants do, **tw** is considered here to be a replacement for **kw** before front vowels. In other words, **tw** and **kw** are different pronunciations of the same basic consonant. In the discussion of vowel harmony, it was shown that present-day **gya** is derived from **gia** (page 21), and it seems reasonable to derive **twa** 'cut' from **kwia**, that is, the palatal articulation of **tw** is due to the influence of the following high front vowel **i**. The occurrence of **tw** before back rounded vowels as in the examples above, is due to a phonological process in Akan in which labialised consonants and final **w** cause front unrounded vowels to be back and rounded, as illustrated by the two pronunciations **twuw/ twiw** for the word for 'push' in Akuapem and Fante. (See Chapter 6, rounding of vowels.)

14. **dw** as in dwi(riw)/dwuruw 'pull down'

This is a labialised voiced pre-palatal affricate. **dw** is articulated further forward on the palate than **gy**. Like **tw** the lip-rounding is of the labial -palatalisation type.

dw occurs before front and back vowels, as in the examples below.

dwen(e)	'think'	dwi(riw)/ dwuruw	'pull down'
dwom	'song'	adwuma	'work'

dw occurs before **a** in Asante, where it corresponds to **gu** in Akuapem and Fante, as in the following examples.

As: dware	'have a bath'	Ak.Fa : guarɛ
odwan	'sheep'	oguan / iguan

There are however a few words in Akuapem where **dw** occurs before **a**, e.g. dwaɛ 'haughtiness'.

As noted under **gu**, **dw** and **gu** generally complement each other in their distribution, and like **tw** and **kw** they are considered here as different pronunciations of the same basic consonant.

In Akuapem and Asante **dw** is replaced by **nw** [ɲɥ] when it occurs after a nasal in the same word.

ndwom 'songs' pronounced [ɲɲɥom /ɲɲɥõm]

37

ndwene   'not think'   pronounced [ɲɲɥɛ̃nɛ̃]

Nasals

15. **m** as in   ma 'give'.
     This is a voiced bilabial nasal.
A labial-palatalised **m** occurs in Asante :

      mua   'close / shut'   pronounced   [mɥɪ̄ā]

In Fante **m** is palatalised before front vowels:

      men 'swallow'   pronounced   [myɛ̃n]

m is the only consonant that occurs in word-final position in all dialects.

      pam 'sew'   **som** 'serve'

It also occurs before other labial consonants:

      mpa 'bed'   **mba** 'children' (Fa)   **mmu** 'not break'

     In Akuapem and Asante **m** may correspond to **b** that occurs after a nasal.

      mba 'children'   pronounced   **mma**

      mbu 'not break' pronounced   **mmu**

16. **n** as in   nom 'drink'
     This is a voiced alveolar nasa...
     n is labial-palatalised in the following words:

      nua [nɥɪ̄ā]   'sibling'   **noa** [nɥɛ̃ā] 'cook' (Fa)

n does not occur before front vowels in Fante. It is replaced by **ny** in this position, as illustrated below:

    Ak. As: nim   'know'   Fa: nyim

        onipa   'human'   nyimpa

          ne   'and'   nye

38

The few instances where **n** occurs before front vowels in Fante are in the Past Tense forms of the verb, and in the 3rd person singular possessive pronoun.

ɔtɔnee   'he sold it'   ne /ni   'his/ her'

Only in Fante does **n** occur in word-final position. Such words either end in **n** followed by a high vowel in Akuapem and Asante, or end in **ŋ** in Akuapem; and in Asante, there is a tongue movement from the vowel towards **ŋw** or **ny** depending on whether the preceding vowel is a back or a non-back vowel respectively, as illustrated by the following examples.

Fa : pen	'agree'	Ak : pene	As : pene
kan	'read'	kaŋ	kany
tɔn	'sell'	tɔŋ	tɔŋw

(see Chapter 4, CVn(V) stems, for a more detailed description of these forms)

n occurs before other alveolar consonants, as in

nsu   'water'   ntama/ntoma 'cloth'
nnom   'not drink'   nda   'days' (Fa)

In Akuapem and Asante **n** may correspond to **d** that occurs after a nasal.

nda   'days'   pronounced nna
ndi   'not eat' pronounced nni

17. **ny** [ɲ] as in **nya** 'have / obtain'
    This is a voiced palatal nasal.
    ny occurs before front vowels and **a**, and never before back vowels.

nyin   'grow'   nya   'have /obtain'

It also occurs before other palatal consonants, and before **h** when it is followed by a front vowel. It is normally spelt with **n** in this position:

nyi   'not remove'   nkye   'not catch'
nhyɛ   'not wear'   nhia   'not need'

39

In Fante **ny** corresponds to three different sounds in Akuapem and Asante - **ny, n, y**, as in

Ak. As:	nyin	'grow'	Fa:	nyin
	nim	'know'		nyim
	yam	'grind'		nyam

In Akuapem and Asante **ny** may correspond to **gy** that occurs after a nasal.

ngye	'not receive'	pronounced	nnye
ngyina	'not stand'	pronounced	nnyina

18. **nw** [ɲɥ] as in nwini / nwunu 'shade'

This is a labialised voiced palatal nasal. The place of articulation for this sound is further forward on the palate than it is for **ny** and the lip-rounding is of the labial-palatalisation type.

In Akuapem and Fante, **nw** only occurs before front vowels.

nwini 'shade' nwene 'weave'

In Asante such words may be pronounced with either front or back vowels if the stem is made up of two syllables in which the second syllable consists of **n** followed by a high vowel. (See Chapter 6, rounding of vowels, for a fuller discussion.)

	nwini /nwunu	'shade'	nwene /nwono 'weave'
but	nwiinwii	'grumble'	

In Fante **nw** corresponds to two sounds in Akuapem and Asante - **nw** [ɲɥ] and **w** [ɥ], as in

Ak.As:	nwini /nwun	'shade'	Fa:	nwin
	wɛn	'watch'		nwɛn

In Akuapem and Asante **nw** [ɲɥ] may correspond to **dw** that occurs after a nasal in the same word.

| ndwom | 'songs' | pronounced | [ɲɲɥom / ɲɲɥ̃õm] |
| ndwene | 'not think' | pronounced | [ɲɲɥẽnẽ̀] |

19. **n** [ŋ] as in **nkɔ** [ŋkɔ] 'not go'

This is a voiced velar nasal. It is spelt with **n**.

[ŋ] does not occur as the initial consonant in a stem. It usually occurs before velar consonants and before **h** when it is followed by a non-front vowel, as in the following examples.

    nka   'not say'   **ngo(w)** 'not soft' (Fa)   **nhu**   'not see'

On account of the very limited distribution of [ŋ], and the fact that the other velar consonants **k g** pattern with palatal consonants **ky, gy**, it is considered here that like **k** and **ky**; **g** and **gy**, the velar nasal [ŋ] and the palatal nasal **ny** should be grouped together as different pronunciations of the same basic consonant.

In the Akuapem dialect [ŋ] occurs in final position, e.g. **kaŋ** 'read'. (see **n** above for the equivalent in the other dialects)

In Akuapem and Asante [ŋ] may correspond to **g** which occurs after a nasal in the same word, as in

    ngo(w)   'not soft'   pronounced [ŋŋo(w) / ŋŋọw]

20. **nw** [ŋw] as in **nwansi** 'sneeze'

This is a labialised voiced velar nasal.

As a stem-initial consonant **ŋw** occurs before **a** in a few words only

    ɔnwam   'a large bird'   **nwansi**   'sneeze'

It occurs before the back vowel **ọ** in the prefix of the following reduplicated form

    nwonwa / nwanwa   'wonderful'

It also occurs before labialised back (i.e. velar and glottal) consonants,

    nwu   'not die'   **nhua**   'not beg for food'

    nkwan   'soup'   **nguan**   'sheep'

nw [ɲɥ] and [ŋw] complement each other in their distribution in so far as ŋw occurs before **a** and ɲɥ occurs before other vowels, and like **kw** and **tw**; **gu** and **dw**; **ŋw** and **ɲɥ** are considered different pronunciations of the same basic consonant, or members of the same phoneme.

In Akuapem **ŋw** may correspond to **gu** that occurs after a nasal in the same word.

nguan 'sheep'   pronounced [ŋŋwuaŋ]

Lateral

21. **l** as in lɔɔre 'lorry'
   This is a voiced alveolar lateral.
   l occurs mainly in loan words such as 'lorry', ball'. It also occurs between vowels in some subdialects of Fante and Asante as an alternative for **r**, and sometimes for **d** as well. In Fante, the alternation is limited to certain words only. In Asante, it is more general, although it is considered substandard.

Fa : ɔlɛ /ɔrɛ /ɔdɛ   'he says'

As : akɔlaa /akɔraa /akɔdaa 'child'

(**l** occurs in some of the other Akan dialects, such as Bron and Kwahu, eg. Bron: ɔlɛ/ɔrɛ/ɔdɛ 'he says'; Kwahu: ɔlɛkɔ 'he's going').

Trill /Frictionless continuant (approximant)

22. **r** as in ɔreba 'he's coming'
   This sound is a voiced alveolar trill in the speech of some Akuapem speakers, and a frictionless continuant in Fante and Asante. **r** occurs in intervocalic position (i.e. between vowels), and after other consonants :

meresɔre   'I am getting up'   pra   'sweep'

As indicated above, **r** and **l** are used interchangeably in some sub-dialects of Fante and Asante, and it also alternates with **d**.
   Like **n**, it is only in Fante that **r** occurs in word-final position. In the other dialects, **r** in such words is always followed by a vowel.

| Fa: hor | 'wash' | Ak. As: horo |
| ker | 'weigh' | kari |

r never occurs as the initial consonant in a stem word, that is, there are no verb stems, nouns or adjectives that begin with **r**. It however occurs in word-initial position in Progressive forms of the verb in Akuapem and Fante. In Asante the Progressive prefix is realised as a lengthening of the preceding vowel, so there are no words in Asante that begin with **r**.

Kofi **reba** (Ak.Fa.)   As: Kofiiba   'Kofi is coming'

On the other hand **d** occurs mainly in stem-initial position, so that **d** and **r** complement each other in their distribution, since **d** occurs mainly in stem-initial position, and **r** mainly in stem-medial position. Moreover **r** alternates with **d** in intervocalic position in some dialects, and **d** , **r**, as well as **l** are regarded here as members of the same phoneme, that is, different pronunciations of the same basic consonant.

Fricatives

23. **f** as in fa 'take'
This is a voiceless labio-dental fricative.
f occurs before all vowels, as in

fie   'home'   fa   'take'   fɔw   'wet'

In Fante **f** is palatalised before front vowels.

fɛm   'borrow /lend'   pronounced [fyɛ̃m]

24. **s** as in se 'teeth'
This is a voiceless alveolar fricative.
A palatalised [sy], spelt **si**, occurs before **a** as in siane 'descend'; and a labial-palatalised [sɥ] occurs in sua 'learn' pronounced [sɥɪ̄ā].
There is also a labialised **s**, spelt **su**, in the articulation of which the tongue assumes the position for **u**. It occurs before **a** in sua 'be small'. Lip-rounding for this consonant is more like what occurs in labial-palatalisation than in plain labialisation, but the tongue shape is slightly different. The tongue assumes the position for the **u** vowel during the articulation of **su**, but not of **sɥ**, where the tongue is much fronter and

43

closer to the palate. It was pointed out in the section on vowel harmony (page 21) that only advanced vowels occur before this consonant, and that it may be said to be articulated with advanced tongue root position.

s , **si** and **su** contrast before **a** in a few words.

      sa 'be finished'   **sia** 'be hanging /suspended'   **sua** 'be small'

25. **hy** as in **hyɛ** 'wear'
This is a voiceless pre -palatal (alveolo-palatal) fricative.
hy occurs before oral front vowels only, as in

      hyire(w) 'white clay'   **hye(w)** 'burn'

h occurs before all the other vowels, so that **hy** and **h** complement each other in their distribution. (See below under **h** .)

26. **hw** as in **hwie** 'pour out'
This is a labialised pre-palatal fricative. It has the same place of articulation as the labial- palatal glide/semivowel [ɥ] as in **owia** 'sun', but **hw** is voiceless, and there is no evidence that there is friction at the lips during the articulation of this sound. This is why it is not described as a voiceless labial-palatal fricative.
hw occurs before front vowels only, as in

      hwe   'beat up'   **hwɛ**   'look at'

Unlike **hy, hw** occurs before nasalised front vowels.

      nwẽnẽ 'nose'   **nhwĩ** 'hair'
(also pronounced **nwẽnẽ, nwĩ**)

In these words **hw** is nasalised, and it does not sound as fricative as when it occurs before oral vowels.
In Asante only, nasalised **hw** occurs before nasalised **a**, as in

      hua 'beg for food'   **huam** 'be sweet scented'

In Akuapem and Fante the corresponding consonant is **hu**, (28) below.

44

27. **h** as in ɛha 'here'

This is a voiceless glottal fricative. During the articulation of **h**, the tongue assumes the position for the following vowel, so that the front of the tongue is raised during the articulation of **h** in hia 'need', and the back of the tongue is raised during the articulation of **h** in huru 'to boil'. Before nasalised vowels **h** is nasalised.

h occurs before back vowels, the central vowel **a**, and nasalised front vowels. In other words it occurs in all the positions where **hy** does not occur.

hu(w)	'blow air'	hare	'be light in weight',
hĩ	'wear out /become thin'	hẽm	'to blow one's nose'

h and **hy** complement each other in their distribution, that is, **hy** replaces **h** before oral front vowels, and they are members of the same phoneme.

28. **hu** as in huam 'be sweet scented' (Ak. Fa.)

This is a labialised glottal fricative during which the back of the tongue assumes the position for the advanced high back vowel **u**, so that it is articulated with advanced tongue root position. **hu** is nasalised, and it occurs only before nasalised **a** in a few words in the Akuapem and Fante dialects.

huã	'beg for food'	huãm	'be sweet scented'

hu does not occur in Asante. The corresponding sound in Asante is **hw**.

hw and **hu** complement each other in their distribution: **hw** before front vowels only, **hu** before **a**. Like other labialised back consonants and the corresponding labialised palatal consonants such **kw** and **tw**, **gu** and **dw**, **hu** and **hw** are considered members of the same phoneme. (**Note**: a plain labialised [hw], that is without advanced tongue root, occurs in the Asante word for 'who' pronounced [hwãẽ], Ak: hɛna, Fa: wọana. This is the only instance in which this consonant is known to occur in Akan.)

Semivowels (glides)

29. **w** as in ɔwɔ 'snake'

This is a labial-velar semivowel.

w occurs before back vowels and the central vowel **a**.

wu	'die'	wɔ	'to pound'	ware	'marry'

In the Akuapem and Fante dialects, **w** occurs in word-final position.

saw	'dance'	hyew	'bum'	dɔw	'weed'

(As: sa, hye, dɔ).

In Asante **w** occurs in word-final position only in the words ɔhaw 'troubles', Yaw 'name of a boy born on Thursday', and kyɛw 'hat' in the expression mepa wo kyɛw 'please' (literally: I remove my hat to you).

Like other semivowels **w** does not occur before or after nasalised vowels. The vowels in the examples above are all oral.

30. **w** [ɥ] as in owia 'sun'
This is a labial-palatal semivowel.
[ɥ] occurs before front vowels only.

wie	'finish'	we	'chew'	wɛn	'watch'

[ɥ] and **w** complement each other in their distribution - [ɥ] replaces **w** before front vowels. They are therefore members of the same phoneme.

In Asante, there is one exception where [ɥ] occurs before a back vowel in the word yɔ pronounced [ɥɔ] 'do'.

Like other semivowels [ɥ] does not occur before nasalised vowels.

In Fante, **nw** [ɲɥ] before a nasalised vowel sometimes corresponds to [ɥ] in Akuapem and Asante.

Fa:	nwɛ̃n	'watch'	Ak. As. :	wɛn

31. **y** as in yi 'remove'
This is a palatal semivowel.
y occurs mainly before front vowels and **a.**

yere	'wife'	yɛn	'to rear'	yam	'to grind'

It also occurs before back vowels in a few words.

| ɔyɔnko | 'friend' | yoo | very well' (expression of agreement) |
| yoma | 'camel' | yuu | ideophone referring to the movement of a mass of people, animals, etc. in one direction. |

Like the other semivowels, **y** does not occur before nasalised vowels.
In Fante only, **ny** before a nasalised vowel sometimes corresponds
to **y** in Akuapem and Asante.

| Fa: | nyɛ̄n | 'to rear' | Ak. As : | yɛn |
| | nyām | 'to grind' | | yam |

B   Summary of consonant distribution.

The main features of consonant distribution in Akan
may be summed up as follows :

1.   Labial and alveolar consonants occur before all vowels - front, back,
central - (except where indicated for Fante **t, d, n, ts, dz**).

2.   Non-labialised palatal consonants, e.g. **ky, hy,** occur mainly before
front vowels, and are in complementary distribution with non-labialised
back consonants - velar and glottal consonants **k, g , ŋ ,h** - which occur
mainly before back vowels and **a**.

3.   Labialised palatal consonants, e.g. **tw, nw,** occur mainly before front
and back vowels, and are on the whole in complementary distribution with
the labialised back consonants **kw, gu, ŋw, hu** , which occur only
before **a**.   The two sets of consonants however contrast before **a** in a
few words. As pointed out in the relevant places, the labialised palatal
consonants are articulated further forward on the palate than the
non-labialised palatal consonants.

4.   All consonants, except **r** and **ŋ** , occur in stem-initial position.

5.   Nasals occur before other consonants, where they are homorganic
with (i.e.have the same place of articulation as) the following consonant,
e.g. **mpa** 'bed, **nsu** 'water', **ŋka** 'not say'.

6.   Only a few consonants occur in word-final position: **m** (all dialects), **w**
(Ak. Fa.), **ŋ** (Ak), **n, r** (Fa).

7. Semivowels in Akan occur in the environment of oral vowels only.

On the basis of their distribution, Akan consonants may be grouped as follows. The consonants in brackets are more or less in complementary distribution with the preceding consonants.

	Labial	Alveolar	Back non-labialised	Back labialised
Plosive	p	t (ts)	k (tɕ)	kw (tɕɥ)
	b	d (dz, r, l)	g (dʑ)	gu (dʑɥ)
Nasal*	m	n	ŋ (ɲ)	ŋw (ɲɥ)
Fricative	f	s	h (ɕ)	hu (ɕɥ)
Semivowel			y	w (ɥ)

* For a further statement on the classification of nasals see Chapter 4.

IV THE GLOTTAL STOP

The glottal stop is the sound made in the larynx or voice box when one holds one's breath for a short period and releases the closure suddenly. It is represented by the symbol [ʔ].

The glottal stop is not part of the consonant system of Akan, and is therefore not included in the consonant chart. It however occurs in spoken Akan, and that is why it is considered necessary to discuss it here. Many Akan speakers are not aware of it, although there are at least two words in the language which are distinguished mainly by the presence or absence of the glottal stop. The words are tɔ 'to buy', and tɔ [tɔʔ] 'to die in tragic circumstances', a word that is better known in the form ɔtɔfo 'the ghost of someone who dies in an accident' etc. The

sentences ɔatɔ 'he has bought it', and ɔatɔʔ 'he has died suddenly/
tragically' (As.), are different only in the presence of the glottal stop in
ɔatɔʔ and its absence in ɔatɔ.

The following is a summary of the contexts in which the glottal stop is
known to occur. Younger Akan speakers use the glottal stop in fewer
contexts than do older speakers.

A   Phonetic contexts

i) The glottal stop occurs only at the end of a word that is followed by
pause.

	kɔʔ	'go!'	pamʔ	'sew it'
but	kɔ fie	'go home'	pam atade no	'sew the dress'

The glottal stop is therefore a feature of pause in Akan.

ii) It occurs after syllables that end in

1. a short vowel :

	kɔʔ	'go!'		faʔ	'take it'
but	kɔɔ	'red'		tie	'listen'

2. a final consonant :

nomʔ	'drink it'
ɔsawʔ	'he dances (well)' (Ak.Fa.)
ɔatɔŋʔ/ɔatɔnʔ	'he has sold it' (Ak.Fa.)
ɔfɛrʔ	'he is shy' (Fa.)

It is worth pointing out that these words that end final short vowels
or final consonants are all words that have been reduced from longer
stems.

huʔ	from	hunu	'see'
sawʔ	from	sawo	'dance'
fɛrʔ (Fa)	from	fɛre	'laugh'
nomʔ	from	nomo	'drink'
danʔ/daŋʔ	from	dane	'turn over'

kɔ 'go' for example ends in **r** in its base form, as reflected in

Fa: ɔkɔree   'he went'

As: me na merekorɔ no 'I (emphatic) am going

It may be concluded from this that tɔ 'to buy' which is not followed by a glottal stop in pre-pausal position is not a reduced form, but that tɔ 'to die tragically' is a reduced form, as reflected in the Fante form   ɔtɔree 'he died suddenly/tragically'.
(See Chapter 4, CVSV stems, for a fuller discussion of these stems.)

B   Grammatical contexts

Within the limitations set by the phonetic context, there are certain grammatical structures in which the glottal stop is known to occur or not occur.

i) It occurs after negative sentences.

ɔantɔ?	'he did not buy it'
ɔnte ha?	'he does not live here'
mengye bi?	'I don't accept /receive some of it'
ɔnyɛ tikya?	'he isn't a teacher'
onhu me?	'he doesn't see me'

ii) It does not occur after interrogative sentences.

ɔkɔ	'has he gone?'
ɔantɔ	'didn't he buy it?'
ɔnte ha	'doesn't he live here?'
ɔnyɛ tikya	'isn't he a teacher?'
onhu me	'doesn't he see me?'

iii) It does not occur after the definite and indefinite articles nʊ, bi, or after personal pronouns   me, wo, wɔn, etc. 'I', 'you', 'they'; or after the locatives ha, hɔ 'here', 'there', except where these words occur at the

50

end of a negative sentence, as in the examples above.

In other contexts the use of the glottal stop is irregular, that is, a speaker may or may not use the glottal stop in such contexts.

CHAPTER 3

TONE

I   INTRODUCTION

Akan is a tone language, which means that the meaning of a word in Akan depends not only on the vowels and consonants of which the word is made, but also on the relative pitch on which each syllable of the word is pronounced. In the following examples the tone marks are (´) for High tone, said on a relatively high pitch, and (`) for Low tone, said on a relatively low pitch.

(a)	pápá	'good'	pàpá	'father'	pàpà	'fan'
(b)	dá	'day'	dà	'never'		
(c)	ɔbɔfó	'hunter'	ɔbɔ́fó	'creator'		

Pitch refers to the musical level on which a sound is said. It is related to the rate at which the vocal cords vibrate: a fast vibration of the vocal cords gives an auditory sensation of high pitch, and a slow vibration, low pitch.

The syllable is the tone-bearing unit in Akan, and it is therefore important to determine what constitutes a syllable in the language.

II   THE SYLLABLE IN AKAN

The syllable structure of a language is generally stated in terms of the consonants, C, and the vowels, V, that make it up. In Akan the syllable is also described in terms of the tone on which the consonant and/or vowel which make up the syllable are uttered.

The following syllable types occur in Akan :

1.	V : ɔ́, ɔ̀	in	ɔ́-fà / ɔ̀-fá	'he takes it'
	è	in	tì-è	'listen'
	ò , ì	in	ò-hú-ì	'he saw it' (Ak.Fa.)

52

2. CV :kɔ́   'go'

    tì   in tì-è   'listen'

    bì, sá in ò-bì-sá   'he asks'

3. C : ǹ   in ǹ-sú   'water'

    ḿ   in sò-ḿ   'hold it'

    ŋ́   in ɔ̀-dà-ŋ́   'he turns it over' (Ak.)

    ǹ   in ɔ̀-dá-ǹ   'he turns it over' (Fa.)

    ŕ   in ɔ̀-fɛ̀-ŕ   'he is shy' (Fa.)

When a syllable is made up of a consonant only, as in (3) above, the consonant is referred to as a syllabic consonant, and it is tone-bearing, that is, it has its own tone.

It follows from the above description of Akan syllable structure that

a)   Akan does not have a syllable that ends in a consonant, that is, there are no VC or CVC syllable types in Akan. Every final consonant constitutes a separate syllable with a tone of its own, whether this tone is different from that of the vowel that precedes it, as in the examples above, or whether it is the same as the tone of the preceding vowel, as in some of the following examples.

    dà-ǹ   'turn it over'

    ɔ̀-dá-ǹ / ɔ̀-dà-ŋ́   'he turns it over' (Fa.Ak.)

    ɔ́-sà-ẁ ǹsú   'she collects water' (Ak.Fa.)

    ɔ̀-sá-ẁ ǹsú   'she collected water' (Ak.Fa.)

    kyɛ́-ŕ   'delay / keep long' (Fa.)

    ɔ̀kyɛ́-ŕ hɔ́   'he kept long there' (Fa.)

    ká-ń   'read it'

    ɔ̀-ká-ǹ/-ŋ́ ǹhómá   'he read a book' (Ak.Fa.)/'he reads a book'(As)

b)   Every vowel in Akan constitutes a syllable, and each vowel in a vowel sequence belongs to a different syllable, whether the vowels are said on different pitches or not, and whether the vowels are of the same quality or not.

tî-è / tsî-è	'listen'
ò-tî-é	'he listens' (Ak. As.)
ò-tsé-ì	'he listens' (Fa.)
mè-è	'be full /eat enough'
ɔ-mè-é	'he eats enough'

c)   There are no CCV syllables in Akan. Words like frɛ 'call', pra 'sweep' are analysed as two syllables. The structure of these words is discussed in detail under CVrV stem structures in Chapter 4. For the moment it is enough to point out that such words are pronounced with a high front vowel between the two consonants when a speaker is speaking slowly or emphatically.

kyerɛ	'show/ teach'	pera	'sweep'
firi	'buy on credit'	bere	'be red'

This pronunciation is reflected in the spelling of some of these words, as in the examples above, except pera 'sweep', which is spelt without the first vowel letter.

When the first vowel is not pronounced, r carries the tone of the first syllable, and it is a syllabic consonant in such words, in other words it belongs to a different syllable from that of the following vowel.

ɔkyèré	or	ɔkyré	'he shows/teaches'
mèpèraê	or	mèpraê	'I swept' (Ak.As.)
òfìrí	or	òfrí	'he buys on credit' (Ak.As.)
compare Fa: òfìr̂			'he buys on credit'

The last two examples show how in Akuapem and Asante syllabic r carries the tone of the first vowel which is not pronounced, while in Fante it carries the tone of the second vowel which is not pronounced. Akan CCV stems such as pra are therefore two syllable words which are derived from CVCV forms, hence the exclusion of CCV in the list of syllable types.

III THE BASIC TONES

Akan is a register tone language in which the two basic tones, High tone and Low tone, are pronounced on relatively level pitch.

A High tone

High tone is usually pronounced on a relatively high level pitch. Where High tone occurs in utterance-final position in an interrogative sentence requiring the answer 'yes' or 'no', that final High tone has a slight fall in pitch. Such interrogative sentences are normally said on a higher pitch over the whole utterance than non-interrogative ones. In the examples below the pitch patterns of the sentences are represented between two parallel lines in which the top line stands for high pitch and the bottom line, low pitch.

ὲwɔ̀ Kòfí hɔ́ ?		'does Kofi have it?'
compare		
ὲwɔ̀ Kòfí nɔ́		'Kofi has it/ it is with Kofi'

Two adjacent High tones may either

    i) have the same pitch, as in

        pápá 'good'   yéré   'wife'

or

    ii) the second High tone may have a slightly lower pitch than that of the first High tone, as in

        áldéń 'why'   ɔbɔ́ʰfó 'messenger'

The second High tone in these examples is called a Downstepped High tone, and is symbolised by an exclamation mark (!) before the syllable that has the Downstepped High tone.

The Downstepped High tone was referred to in earlier studies as a Mid tone, but unlike Mid tone in other languages, it occurs only after another High tone, and never after a Low tone or in word-initial position. Moreover it is often predictable, especially in longer utterances where a sequence of High tones are separated by one or more Low tones. Although it contrasts with High tone in Akan, as in

55

ɔbɔfó   'creator'   ɔbɔ!fó   'messenger'

it is now considered more appropriate to describe it as a variant of the High tone. The Downstepped High tone is therefore a High tone which is lower in pitch than a preceding High tone. Where, as in the examples given so far, the Downstepped High tone is not predictable from the context, the Downstep symbol (!) is used.

B   Low tone

Low tone is usually said on a relatively low level pitch. As noted above, 'Yes/No' questions are normally said on a higher pitch range than statements, and this affects the pitches of Low tones in such utterances. However the difference in pitch range between an interrogative sentence and a non-interrogative sentence is less pronounced for utterances that have Low tones only, as in the example below, than it is for utterances that have High tone.

(a) ɔsɛ̀ àdò   _____   'does he look like Addo?'
                       _ _ _ _

(b) ɔsɛ̀ àdò   _____   'he looks like Addo'
                       _ _ _ ＿

Successive Low tones are normally said on the same pitch. However, where they are utterance-final, the pitch steadily drops on each subsequent Low tone, and the final Low tone has a slight fall in pitch, as in sentence (b) above.

IV   DOWNDRIFT

A   Automatic Downstep

In Akan a Low tone tends to lower the pitch of a following High tone, so that in a High-Low-High sequence, the second High tone is downstepped, that is, it is lower in pitch than the first one, as illustrated below.

$$H - L - H ----> H - L - !H$$

                       _____
                         _   _
as in   Kòfí pàpá   _   __ ＿   'Kofi's father'

In an utterance with a succession of Low-High sequences therefore, there is a gradual drop in the pitches of the High tones from the beginning of the utterance to the end, and a final High tone in a long utterance can have a lower pitch than a Low tone at the beginning of the utterance. The pitch of a Low tone that precedes a High tone is also raised, although the pitch raise is not comparable to the pitch drop that occurs on the High tone. This steady drop in the pitches of High tones preceded by Low tones in an utterance is called Downdrift, and is a feature of intonation in Akan. The lowered High tones are referred to as automatic Downstep, since the Low tone that lowered the pitch of the High tone is evident. The Downstep symbol (!) is therefore not used. Sentences (1) to (3) below illustrate this point.

(1) Kòfí pàpá rèkàsá
     'Kofi's father is speaking' (Ak.As.)

(2) pàpá Kòfí rèfrɛ́ nè bá
     'Papa Kofi is calling his child' (Ak.As)

(3) pàpá Kòfí rèfrɛ́ né bá
     'Papa Kofi is calling his child' (Fa.)

Note that in (3), the Fante version of sentence (2), the three final syllables are on the same pitch because they are all High tone, not High-Low-High as in (2), the Akuapem and Asante sentence.

In general the downdrift pattern extends over the clause, as shown in the following sentence, (4), where each of the three clauses has a separate downdrift pattern. In such a long sentence the first High tone of a non-initial clause is normally lower in pitch than that of the preceding clause, so that there is an overall downdrift pattern over the whole sentence

(4) pàpá Kòfí kàsá kyèrɛ́ nè bá sɛ̂ ɔ́mfá ádàm̀fò pá

     nà wàsùá ádè pá bí áfì nò ǹkyɛ́ń

'Papa Kofi tells his child that he should make friends with a good person so that he can learn something good from him.'

57

1. Sometimes the Low tone in a H-L-H sequence is assimilated to the pitch of the preceding High tone, that is, the pitch of the preceding High tone spreads to the following syllable, and replaces the pitch of the Low tone. However, the pitch lowering effect that the Low tone has on the following High tone remains, and the second High tone is downstepped, that is,

$$H - L - H \longrightarrow H - L - !H \longrightarrow H - H - !H$$

In the following examples of noun phrases, the tone pattern of the citation form of each word is given first, to the left, and the pronunciation of the whole phrase, showing the assimilated Low tone, is given to the right.

(5) Kòfí, ǹsú(ó)   --->   Kòfí ńsú(ó)   'Kofi's water'

(6) `Afúá, m̀pá    ---->    `Afúá ḿlpá   'Afua's bed'

(7) Kòfí, `Adú   --->   Kòfí áldú   'a boy's name'

(8) sàá, ònípá yí   ---->   sàá ólnípá yì   'this person'

The Low tone that is assimilated to the pitch of a preceding High tone usually occurs on nominal prefixes, as in the examples above, and on the prefix **a-** of the Perfect form of the verb, as in the following sentences.

(9) Kòfí, àbá   ---->   Kòfí álbá   'Kofi has come' (As.)

(10) Kòfí álbɛká álkyérɛ́ pàpá   ' Kofi has come & told father' (Ak.As.)

The pitch levels of the High tones in the sentence above show why the term Downstepped High tone is considered more appropriate than the older term Mid tone, since the three 'Mid tone' levels in this sentence are all derived from High tones.

In Asante possessive constructions the Low tone that is assimilated in the H - L - H sequence may occur on the first syllable of a stem, or on both the prefix and the first syllable of the stem, as illustrated below.

| sìká | but | Kòfí sí lká | 'Kofi's money' |
| ǹtòmá | but | pàpá ńtólmá | 'father's cloth' |

2. Sometimes the Low tone syllable in a H-L-H sequence may be deleted, that is dropped altogether, but its pitch lowering effect on the following High tone remains, that is,

$$\text{H - L - H} \longrightarrow \text{H - L - !H} \longrightarrow \text{H - !H}$$

(11) Kòfí, ɔdáń   ---->   Kòfí !dáń   'Kofi's house'

(12) né, ɔbó   ---->   né !bó   'it's price'

(13) sàá, ònípá yí   ---->   sàá !nípá yí   'this person'

(14) Kòfí, ɔàbéká, ɔàkyéré ḿ ---> Kòfí !ábéká !ákyéré ḿ

            'Kofi has come and told me (Fa.)'

As can be seen from the last sentence, the Perfect prefix is said on High tone in Fante, and this High tone syllable is downstepped when the Low tone pronoun prefix is dropped, hence the tonal difference between this Fante sentence and the Akuapem and Asante sentence (10).

V DOWNSTEPPED HIGH TONE

The above shows that Downtepped High tone may be

A Lexical, that is, part of the basic structure of a word:

(15)   àdá!ká   'box'   yá!w   'grief'

   á!déń   'why' (Ak.As.)   ɔkɔ́!tɔ́   'crab'

B Derived, that is, a result of Downdrift - the relationship between sequences of High and Low tones. There are two types of derived Downstepped High tones:

1. Automatic Downstepped High tone, where the Low tone that lowered the pitch of the following High tone is evident, and therefore the Downstep symbol is not required. In the following sentence, the second High tone on pàpá is downstepped.

(16)   Kòfí pàpá sò   'Kofi's father is big'

2. Non-Automatic Downstepped High tone, where the Low tone that lowered the pitch of a following High tone is not evident because of the

following two reasons:

(i) it has been assimilated to High tone, as in

(17) Kòfí, m̀pá   ---> Kòfí m̄lpá   'Kofi's bed'

(18) Kòfí, àbéfá   ---> Kòfí álbéfá   'Kofi has come for it' (Ak.As)

(ii) it has been deleted, as in

(19) Kòfí, ɔ̀dáń   ---> Kòfí ldáń   'Kofi's house'

(20) Kòfí, ɔ̀ábéfá   ---> Kòfí lábéfá   'Kofi has come for it' (Fa.)

There are therefore three main types of Downstepped High tones in Akan:

Lexical Downstep

Automatic (or Derived) Downstep

Non-Automatic Downstep (or preferably, Downdrifted High tone)

Note that Stewart's (1965) use of the term Non-automatic Downstepped High tone includes Lexical Downstepped High tone.

The examples of Non-automatic Downstepped High tone given so far show tone assimilation or tone spreading across word boundaries. Sometimes the tone spreading occurs across morpheme boundaries (i.e. boundaries between affixes and stems) within a word. For example, in the Future form of the verb, the Future prefix is a High tone syllable bɛ́. When it occurs before a disyllabic Low-High stem, the Low tone of the stem is replaced with High tone, the same pitch as that of the Future prefix.

(21) bɛ́ + bìsá   ---> ɔ̀bébí lsá   'he will ask' (Ak.As.)

Tone spreading is not always from left to right, that is from a preceding High tone to a following Low tone. Sometimes it is the Downstepped High tone in the H-L-!H sequence that spreads to the preceding Low tone, that is.

$$H-L-H \longrightarrow H-L-!H \longrightarrow H-!H-H$$

In Akuapem and Asante, if the second consonant of the disyllabic stem is a sonorant, that is, a nasal or an approximant, the tone spreading in the Future form of the verb is from right to left. In Fante this is true of some of these stems, but not all of them. (See tone of disyllabic stems, Chapter 4.)

stem :	gyìná	(22)	òbélgyíná	'he will stop'
	hòmé	(23)	ɔ̀bélhómé	'he will rest/breathe'
	kyèrɛ́	(24)	ɔ̀bélkyérɛ́	'he will point out'

VI GLIDING PITCHES

The examples so far have been of tones that are said on level pitches. Akan is a register tone language in which the High and Low tones are said on level pitches. Falling and rising pitches do occur however, as explained below.

A Falling pitch

1. When a sequence of High-Low tones occurs on two vowels or on a vowel and a sonorant (nasal or approximant) it is perceived as falling pitch. In a few cases a falling pitch may be a sequence of High- Downstepped High tone, as in (29) below.

(25) ɔ̀faê 'he took it' (Ak.Fa.)

(26) wónkɔ́ 'you don't go' (Ak.As.)

(27) ɔ̀sɔ́r̂ 'he gets up' (Fa.)

(28) ɔ̀nípá aâ 'the person who'

(29) yá꜖ẃ / yélá 'grief'

Note: The relative particle is usually spelt with one vowel letter, **a**, but is pronounced as a long vowel, as indicated in example (28).

61

2. Sometimes the falling pitch occurs on one short vowel, so that a complex High-Low tone occurs on one segment only. This occurs in the following contexts:

(a) In **Fante**, when the past Tense verb is not followed by an object or a complement it has a Low tone vowel suffix. When this Low tone suffix occurs after a final high tone vowel of the verb, the resulting High-Low sequence is realised as falling pitch, as in the following examples.

(30) ɔbâè 'he came'   òbìsâè 'he asked'   ɔtɔ̂è 'he bought it'

However, when such Past Tense verbs are followed by an object or a complement, the suffix is deleted, and the final short vowel of the verb is said on falling pitch. This is a slight fall in pitch, as shown below where the falling pitch ends at about the same pitch as the beginning of the following Downstepped High tone.

(31) ɔbâ há   'he came here'

(32) òbìsâ Kòfí   'he asked Kofi'

(33) ɔtɔ̂ né ¡dzé   'he bought his'

These examples show that although the suffix is deleted when the verb is followed by an object, its tone is not deleted, but is tagged on to the final High tone vowel of the verb. This results in a complex HL tone on the final vowel of the stem. The pitch pattern of sentence (31) shows that the second High tone is downstepped because it is the second High tone in a H - L - H sequence. It is worth pointing out that the vowel that carries the complex tone in these sentences is not longer in duration than a short vowel that is said on High or Low tone.

When the verb ends in a consonant, the falling pitch is spread over the consonant and the preceding vowel, as shown below, in the examples to the right.

(34) ɔpámèè 'he sewed it' *but* ɔpám̀ àtàr̀   'he sewed a dress'

(35) ɔkyéwèè 'she fried it' *but* ɔkyéẁ nám̀   'she fried fish'

(36)   Ak : ɔbáè: ɔbáà há.   ɔpámèè: ɔɾám àtàdé

(37)   As : ɔbàè: ɔbàà há.   ɔpàmèè: ɔpàm(òò) àtàdéé

b) In **Asante** when a verb that ends in a vowel is followed by an object or a complement in the Habitual, Progressive, Perfect or Ingressive Imperative forms of the verb, the final vowel of the verb is said on falling pitch. (Ingressive verbs have a prefix bɛ or kɔ to indicate a coming or going, respectively, that is required for the action indicated by the verb stem, e.g. ɔbɛfa 'he comes and takes it')

(38)   ɔrèhyê kyɛ́   'he is putting a hat on'

(39)   ɔbâ Tálkórádé   'he comes to Takoradi'

(40)   màtɔ̂ lɔ́rè   'I've bought a lorry'

(41)   Yàw àbâ Kùmásé   'Yaw has come to Kumasi'

(42)   kɔfâ kàwá nó   'go and take the ring'

These verbs end in High tone when they are not followed by an object or a complement.

(43) ɔrèhyɛ́   'he is putting on'   (44) ɔbá   'he comes'

(45) màtɔ́   'I've bought it'   (46) ɔ̀abá   'he has come'

(47) kɔfá   'go and take it'

It would appear that as an essential part of the grammatical relationship between a Habitual, Progressive, Perfect or Ingressive Imperative form of the verb and its object or complement, a Low tone is required after the verb. This Low tone links to the final High tone of the verb, and brings about the complex HL tone on the final vowel of the verb in the above sentences.

Where the verb ends in a consonant the complex ,HL tone is spread over the consonant and the preceding vowel, as in the examples below. **m** is the only consonant that regularly occurs in final position in Asante.

63

(48) ɔnóm kɔ́fe   'he drinks coffee'

(49) ɔrèpám àtàdéɛ́   'he's sewing a dress'

These verbs end in Low tone in Akuapem and Fante, and there is no difference in the tone of the verb whether or not it is followed by an object.

(50) ɔbà   :   ɔbà Tákóráde   'he comes to Takoradi'

(51) màátɔ   :   màátɔ dáń   'I've bought a house'

In Asante, whenever the final High tone of the verb is a Downstepped High tone, the HL complex tone on the verb is replaced by a Low tone, that is,

$$H - !HL \longrightarrow H - L$$

(52) ɔabá   : Kòfí álbá   :   Kòfí ábà Kùmásé
                                      'Kofi has come to Kumasi'

(53) ɔatɔ   : álmá áltɔ   :   álmá átɔ dáń
                                      'Ama has bought a house'

but

(54)   tíkyà àtɔ   :   tíkyà àtɔ dáń
                                       'Teacher has bought a house'

These examples show that although it is possible to have a complex HL tone on one segment, a vowel, such a complex tone cannot occur if the first part of the complex tone is a Non-automatic Downstepped High tone, although it can occur on a downdrifted High tone, as in example (54) above.

It has not been possible to find a comparable context for a lexical Downstepped High tone to see if that also does not tolerate a complex HL tone. The following sentences are, however, as close as one can get to identical contexts for both the Lexical and Derived Downstep High tones.

(55) ɔbɛhálta   :   ɔbɛháta wɔ àhòmá só
     'he will dry it'   'he will dry it on the line'

(56) pápáyɛ álsá   :   pápáyɛ ásà wɔ wíásé
     'good deeds are over'   'good deeds are over in the world'

(57)	álmá	:	álmá wɔ Tákóráde
			'Ama is in Takoradi'
(58)	Kòfí síĺká	:	Kòfí síĺká wɔ hà
	Kofi's money'		Kofi's money is here'

In examples (55, 56) the Downstepped High tone on the verb stem is replaced with low tone before wɔ, but in (57) the lexical Downstep on Ama is retained, and so is the derived downstep on sika in (58). Words with Lexical Downstep retain their tonal structure in all environments (except in possessive noun phrases in Asante and Fante, page 74). Derived Downstep, on the other hand, may be affected by its environment, as in (55) and (56) above where it is replaced by Low tone. The replacement of derived Downstep by Low tone appears to be unique to verbs, however, since derived Downstep on the noun, síĺká (58), is retained in a similar environment.

Sentences (52) to (57) therefore show why it is necessary to make a three-way distinction between Lexical Downstep, Derived Downstep, and downdrifted High tone.

c) The conjunction sɛ (As.) dɛ (Fa.) meaning 'that', and the comparative and emphatic particles sɛ (Ak.As.), dɛ (Fa.) are said on falling pitch. The vowel is short, and it is not possible to account for the complex tone, except that it is part of the lexical structure of these words.

(59)	mèkàé sɛ̂ / mékáè dɛ̂	'I remember that'
(60)	ɛ́yɛ̀ hú sɛ̂ / dɛ̂	'it is very frightening'
(61)	ɔsò sɛ̂ né wɔ̀fà /	'he is big/fat like his uncle'
	ɔsò tsè dɛ̂ né wɔ̀fà	

B   Rising pitch

When a sequence of Low-High tones occur on two successive vowels or a vowel and a sonorant, this is perceived as rising pitch.

(62)	màáfà		'I've taken it' (Ak.Fa)
(63)	sòḿ		'hold it'

65

(64)　ɔ́fɛr̄　　 $\underline{\diagup}$ 　　　'he is shy' (Fa.)

There is no example of the L-H sequence occurring on a single vowel or consonant.

What has been stated above describes the relationships between the basic High and Low tones of Akan, in other words what has been said about downdrift, lexical and derived Downstepped High tones etc, are in the main common to all dialects. It must be emphasised however, that the tonal differences between the dialects are very complex, more complex than the differences in the vowels and consonants, and it is not possible to deal with all of them here. Such differences are pointed out where they are considered essential to the discussion, as for example in the discussion of the different Tense/Aspect forms of the verb.

VII FUNCTIONS OF TONE IN AKAN

A Lexical function

There are pairs of words in Akan whose meanings are distinguished purely by tone.

(65)	pápá	'good'	(66)	ɔbɔ́lfó	'messenger'
	pàpá	'father'		ɔbɔ́fó	'creator'
	pàpà	'fan'		ɔbɔ̀fó	'hunter'
(67)	dá	'day'	(68)	kólkó	'hill' (Fa.)
	dà	'never'		k̀okò	'chest'

The number of pairs of words in Akan which differ only in tone is however very limited, and this is why it has been possible for Akan to have an orthography in which tones are not marked. It is usually possible to tell the tone and the meaning of a word from the context.

B Grammatical function

There are certain grammatical categories, especially of the verb, and certain grammatical structures that are distinguished by tone, and in Akan

66

the functional load carried by tone is more significant at the level of grammar than at the lexical level.

The Verb

1. Habitual and Stative forms of the verb

The difference between the Habitual and Stative forms of the verb is carried by tone, as illustrated by the following examples.

Habitual	Stative
(69) ɔ̀hyɛ̀ àtàdé / àtàr̂ (Ak.Fa.)	(70) ɔ̀hyɛ̀ àtàdé(ɛ́) / àtàr̂
(71) ɔ̀hyɛ́ àtàdéɛ́ (As.)	'she has a dress on'
'she wears a dress'	
(72) K̀ofí̂ gyìná hɔ́	(73) K̀ofí̂ gyìnà hɔ́
'Kofi stops/stands there'	'Kofi is standing there'

As can be seen from the above examples, where the verb stem is monosyllabic, the difference between the two verbs is carried by the tone of the verb stem in Asante, but by the pronoun prefix in Fante and Akuapem. This means that in Akuapem and Fante the distinction between the Habitual and the Stative forms of the verb is lost when the verb is monosyllabic, and the subject is expressed by a noun, as in (74) below.

(74) á!má hỳɛ àtàdé / àtàr̂   'Ama wears a dress/has a dress on'

compare Asante

(75) á！má hyɛ́ àtàdéɛ́   (76) á!má hyɛ̀ àtàdéɛ́
'Ama wears a dress'   'Ama has a dress on'

2. Habitual Ingressive and Future forms of the verb

The Habitual Ingressive form has a prefix **bɛ** which indicates a movement towards the speaker required before the action indicated by the verb. This prefix is Low tone in Akuapem and Asante, but High tone in Fante. The Future form of the verb is a High tone prefix **bɛ**, and the difference between the two forms of the verb is carried by tone in Akuapem and Asante. In Fante they are identical, as illustrated by the following examples.

Habitual Ingressive	Future
(77) Kòfí bɛ̀fá	(78) Kòfí bɛ́fá
'Kofi comes and takes it'	'Kofi will take it'

compare Fante:

(79) Fa: Kòfí bɛ́fá

'Kofi comes and takes it /Kofi will take it'

3. Habitual Negative and Optative forms of the verb

The Negative prefix is a Low tone nasal consonant, and the Optative prefix is a High tone nasal. The difference between the Habitual Negative and the Optative forms of the verb is carried by tone.

Habitual Negative	Optative
(80) Kòfí ǹkɔ́	(81) Kòfí ńkɔ́
'Kofi does not go'	'let Kofi go'

4. Habitual and Past Tense forms of the verb

As explained on page 62, when a Fante Past Tense verb that ends in a vowel is followed by an object or a complement, the suffix is deleted, so that it is only its tone pattern that distinguishes it from a Habitual form.

Habitual	Past Tense
(82) Kòfí bà há (Fa)	(83) Kòfí bâ há (Fa)
'Kofi comes here'	'Kofi came here'
(84) ɔ̀frɛ́ Kòfí (Fa)	(85) ɔ̀frɛ̀ Kòfí (Fa)
'he calls Kofi'	'he called Kofi'

In all dialects, where the Past Tense verb ends in a consonant the Habitual and Past Tense forms of the verb are distinguished by tone when they are followed by an object or a complement.

(86) ɔ́pàm̀ àtàdé / àtàr̀ (Ak.Fa) (87) ɔ̀pám̀ àtàdé /àtàr̀ (Ak.Fa)

(88) ɔ̀pám̀ àtàdéɛ́ (As) (89) ɔ̀pàm̀ àtàdéɛ́ (As)

'she sews dresses' 'she sewed a dress'

5. The function of tone in the relationship between a verb and its object or complement in Asante has already been discussed. (pages 63 - 64)

6. The Subordinated and non-subordinated verb

When a verb occurs in a subordinate clause it has a different tone pattern from when it occurs in a non-subordinate clause. The subordinate clause marker nó generally has the effect of raising the pitch of preceding Low tone syllables of verbs.

non-Subordinate form	Subordinate form
(90) Kòfí rèbìsá nó (Ak.As)	(91) Kòfí rébìsá nó (Ak.As)
(92) Kòfí rèbísà (Fa)	(93) Kòfí rébí!sá nó (Fa)
'Kofi is asking him'	'while Kofi was asking'

7. Interrogative and non-Interrogative sentences

It has already been noted (pages 55 and 56) that 'Yes/No' questions are said on a higher pitch over the whole utterance than non-interrogative sentences, even though the basic tone pattern is the same.

(94) Kòfí kɔ́ ? (As)

(95) Kòfí kɔ́

(96) Kòfí kɔ̀ ? (Ak.Fa)
'has Kofi gone?'

(97) Kòfí kɔ̀
'Kofi has gone'

When the interrogative particle àná(á) is used, the higher pitch range is optional, and there is no fall in pitch on a final High tone.

(98) Kòfí kɔ́/kɔ̀ ànáá ?   'has Kofi gone?'

Nouns

The basic tone patterns of the noun are discussed in Section VII below. What follows is a discussion of some of the tone changes that nouns undergo.

8. Nouns in possessive constructions

In Akan the tone of a noun when it occurs in a possessive noun phrase may be different from when it occurs in other constructions, as illustrated by the following examples.

(99) ɔhɔlhó(ɔ́) nó kɔ́ /kɔ̀

'the guest/stranger has gone'

(102) K̀ofí Nyàmé sò

'Kofi Nyame is big / fat'

(100) mè hɔ̀hòɔ́ (As) 'my guest'

(101) mé hɔ̀hòé (Fa) 'my guest'

(103) K̀ofí Nyá!méé sò (As)

'Kofi's God is great'

There are some nouns which retain the same tone pattern in all phrase structures, such as pàpá in

(104) pàpá kɔ́ 'father has gone'

(105) K̀ofí pàpá 'Kofi's father'

In general it is possible to distinguish between two groups of nouns on the basis of their tonal behaviour in possessive constructions. This is particularly true of nouns that have a monosyllabic CV structure and those with disyllabic CVC(V) structure but which tonally behave like monosyllabic stems. These are referred to as Type 1 stems in Chapter 4. Stewart (1976) refers to these as having one 'heavy' syllable only. It can be seen in the following Akuapem and Asante examples that where the Low tone prefix of a Class 1 noun is assimilated to High tone by a preceding High tone, or where the prefix is deleted, this does not cause the following High tone to be downstepped, as has been described in the section on Non-automatic Downstep (pages 58 and 59). Class 2 nouns however conform to the basic tonal relationships described in that section.

	Class 1			Class 2	
(106) ǹsá	:	K̀ofí ńsá	(107) ǹsá	:	K̀ofí ńlsá
		'Kofi's hand'			'Kofi's drink'
(108) èséé	:	Kwàbèná sé	(109) èséé	:	Kwàbèná lsé
		'Kwabena's teeth' (As)			'Kwabena's father' (As)
(110) ɛ̀náń	:	K̀ofí náń	(111) ɛ̀nám̀	:	K̀ofí lnám̀
		'Kofi's leg'			'Kofi's meat/fish'
(112) m̀bá	:	`Abèná m̀bá	(113) m̀pá	:	`Abèná m̀lpá
		'Abena's children'			'Abena's bed'

The tonal difference between Class 1 and Class 2 nouns in possessive constructions is maintained in Fante as well, but Fante possessive noun phrases always have the possessive concord marker (possessive pronoun) in addition to the noun, as in

(114) K̀òfí né̄ n̄sá (115) K̀òfí né̄ ǹ!sá
       'Kofi's hand'   'Kofi's drink'

Most Class 1 nouns are inalienable nouns, that is, they refer to parts of the body, while Class 2 nouns are alienable nouns. In Akan, nouns with basic monosyllabic structure show a difference between alienable and inalienable possession.

In Asante this distinction between alienable and inalienable posse - ssion is reflected in the tone of possessive pronouns, Low tone before inalienable nouns (except the word for hair), and High tone before alienable nouns. Akuapem shows this distinction to some extent, but in Fante, possessive pronouns are always said on High tone. The following examples illustrate alienable and inalienable possession in the three dialects.

As: (116) mè tí   'my head'   but (117) mé !dá́ń   'my house'

    (118) yὲn̄ n̄sá   'our hands' but (119) yὲń ǹ!sá   'our drink'

    (120) nè sé́   'his teeth' but (121) né́ !sé́   'his father'

compare

Ak: (122) mè tí   'my head'   (123) mé !dá́ń   'my house'

    (124) né́ sè   'his teeth'   (125) né́ !kyéẃ   'his hat'

Fa: (126) mé́ tsí́r   'my head'   (127) mé́ !dá́ń   'my house'

    (128) né́ sè   'his teeth'   (129) né́ !kyéẃ   'his hat'

The tonal difference in possesive noun phrases that make it necessary to group basic monosyllabic stems into Class 1 and Class 2 nouns is absent in Akuapem and Fante where the possessed noun is a true disyllabic stem, that is with two 'heavy' syllables. Such stems usually have Low-High or Low-Low tone pattern, as illustrated below.

sìká 'money'   kòkò 'chest'   pàpá 'father'   wòfà 'uncle'

As: (130) K̀òfí síḱká   but   (131) K̀òfí pàpá
          'Kofi's money'   'Kofi's father'

    (132) Kwàsí kókò   but   (133) Kwàsí wòfà
          'Kwasi's chest'   Kwasi's uncle'

71

Ak.Fa: (134) Kòfí (né) sìká (135) Kòfí (né) pàpá

(136) Kwàsí (né) kòkò (137) Kwàsí (né) wòfà

As can be seen from the Asante examples, the initial Low tone of the possessed noun in (130), (132) is replaced by High tone of the same pitch as that of the preceding possessor noun. These nouns, like Class 1 nouns, take a Low tone possessive pronoun in Asante, and they will be classified as Class 1 nouns, while those that retain their basic tone pattern, (131), (133), are Class 2 nouns.

Where the Class 1 noun has a Low tone vowel or syllabic nasal prefix, both the prefix and the initial stem syllable are said on High tone.

ǹtòmá	:	(138) Kòfí ńtò!má	'Kofi's cloth'
ànòmàá	:	(139) Kwàsí ánómàá	'Kwasi's bird'

It may be noted here that in Asante kinship nouns that refer to younger relations belong to Class 1 tone group while those that refer to older relations belong to Class 2 tone group.

wòfààsé	:	(140) wò wòfààsé	'your niece / nephew'
nàná	.	(141) mè ná!ná	'my grandchild'
		(142) mé nàná	'my grandparent'
wòfà	:	(143) wó wòfà	'your uncle'

Kinship nouns in Asante exhibit a superior/non-superior distinction that is reflected in the fact that superior nouns can take the ɔ- 3rd person singular possessive pronoun (human) while non-superior nouns cannot.

(144) nè wòfààsé (145) ɔwòfá / né wòfà
      'his niece / nephew'   'his uncle'
(146) nè ná!ná (147) ɔnàná / né nàná
      'his grandchild'   'his grandparent'

As can be seen from (144) and (146), tone raising on the initial Low tone syllable of the noun takes place even when the noun is preceded by a Low tone possessive pronoun.

Possessive relationship between nouns in some related languages such as Igbo, spoken in Nigeria, is indicated by the presence of an associative High tone that occurs between the two nouns. In this anlysis, the tonal relationship between the two elements of the possessive noun phrase in Asante will be accounted for in terms of such an associative High tone. With Class 1 nouns the associative High tone spreads to the final syllable of the possessed noun. Where it is a Class 2 noun, the associative High tone spreads to the initial stem syllable of the possessor noun, as illustrated below.

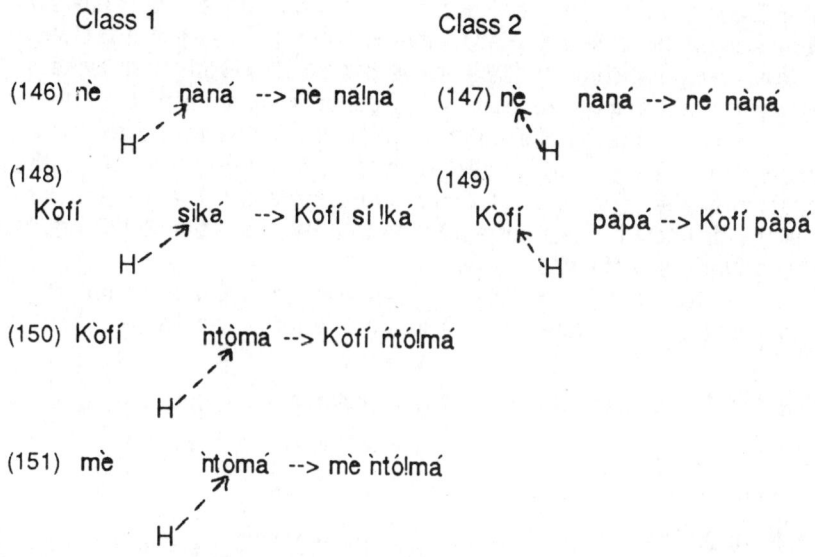

Class 1   Class 2

(146) nè   nàná --> nè ná!ná   (147) nè   nàná --> né nàná

(148)   (149)
   Kòfí   sìká --> Kòfí sí!ká   Kòfí   pàpá --> Kòfí pàpá

(150) Kòfí   ǹtòmá --> Kòfí ǹtó!má

(151) mè   ǹtòmá --> mè ǹtó!má

It can be seen from the above examples that the possessive pronoun is basically Low tone, and that before Class 2 nouns, it takes its High tone from the associative High tone. In (149) the associative High tone has no effect because the possessor noun ends in High tone. As indicated in (148) and (150) the associative High tone spreads to the stem initial syllable of the Class1 noun. The prefix in (150) takes its High tone from the final High tone of the preceding noun, while in (151) the prefix remains Low tone because it is preceded by a Low tone possessive pronoun.

It must be emphasised however, that the above explanation for the tonal relationship between the elements of a possessive noun phrase does not fully account for all the instances of tonal variation that occur in the Asante possessive noun phrase. For example, where the possessor element is a noun and it ends in Low tone, the spreading of the associative High tone is blocked, that is it does not take place whether the noun is Class 1 or Class 2.

	Class 1		Class 2

(152) `Adò, sìká --> `Adò sìká   (153) `Adò pàpá --> `Adò pàpá

'Addo's money'   'Addo's father'

In the above noun phrases, the individual nouns retain their basic tones. Some people however say `Adò síIká for (152). For such speakers normal tone-spreading of the associative High tone takes place for the Class 1 noun. The final Low tone of a possessor noun however never takes on the tone of the associative High tone, as shown in (153).

Another point that must be made is that although there is some justification for having two noun Classes on the basis of their tonal behaviour in the possessive noun phrase, (as illustrated by examples (106) to (113), page 70), these classes are only relevant in the discussion of the tone of possessive noun phrases. In other environments the distinction does not apply, so that the classification of nouns into tonal classes is of limited value.

Where the noun has a Downstepped High tone, the tone pattern of the possessed noun is different in Akuapem, Asante and Fante.

(154)   àdá!ká   'box'   (155)   ɔhɔ́lhó(ɔ́)   'guest'

As :   Kòfí ádákàá   'Kofi's box'   wò hɔhòɔ́   'your guest'

Fa :   Kòfí n'ádàkàé   wó hɔ̀hòé

Ak :   Kòfí á!dá!ká   wó lhɔ́lhó

The Akuapem forms show the normal downstepping resulting from an assimilated (154) or a deleted (155) Low tone. In the Asante and Fante forms the Downstepped High tone is said on Low tone. No attempt will be made to account for the tone changes in these forms. It may however be noted that the Asante forms provide evidence to support the suggestion (e.g. Stewart 1965) that lexical Downstepped High tone, like non-automatic Downstep is traceable to an underlying H-L-H sequence.

9.   Nouns in compounds.

When a noun occurs as the first element in a compound, it is usually said on Low tone whatever its basic tone.

(156)   ɔhéné   'chief'   in   àhìmfíé   'palace'

74

(157)	ɔsálmáń	'ghost'	in	àsàmàmpɔ́ẁ	'burial grove'
(158)	àní	'eye'	in	nìsú(ó)	'tears'
(159)	àsɛ́m̀	'issue'	in	àsɛ̀m̀bìsá	'question'

Compound formation and the tone patterns associated with compounds are discussed in detail in Chapter 5.

10. Tone of nominalised forms

Nominalised forms usually retain the original tone pattern of the verb.

(160)	dɔ́(ẁ)	'to weed'	àdɔ́(ẁ)	'weeding'
(161)	kó	'to fight'	ɔkó	'battle'
(162)	hìá	'to need'	ohìá	'poverty'
(163)	sòmá	'to send on errand'	ɔsòmá	'act of sending people on errands'

There are some Low-High verb stems however which have High-Downstepped High tone in the nominalised form.

(164)	pènè	'to agree'	pélnè	'agreement'
(165)	kàsá	'to speak'	kálsá	'speech / language'
(166)	bìsá	'to ask'	àbí!sá	'consulting juju'
(167)	pàtá	'to pacify'	m̀pá!tá	'pacification'

Given the derivation of non-automatic Downstepped High tone from a H - L - H sequence, it seems plausible to account for the tones of these nominalised forms in terms of a High tone nominalising prefix which occurs before the Low-High stem of the verb. This results in a H - L - H sequence from which the H - !H tone pattern of the noun is derived.

VIII TONE PATTERNS OF THE MAJOR WORD CLASSES

A The Verb

The verb in Akan may have different tone patterns, and this is determined by various factors. The main ones are as follows:

1. the Tense or Aspect in which it occurs (see Appendix I for the full scatter of the Tense/Aspect forms of the verb.)
2. the syllable structure of the verb stem, that is whether it is one syllable (monosyllabic), two (disyllabic), three (trisyllabic), etc. (see Chapter 4)
3. whether or not it is followed by an object or a complement, as illustrated on pages 62 - 64.
4. the type of clause it occurs in, for example, whether it occurs in a subordinate or a main clause, as exemplified on page 69.

The following examples illustrate some of these points.

(a) Monosyllabic : kɔ́   (b) Disyllabic : kyèrɛ́   (c) Disyllabic : bìsá

(168)	kɔ́	kyèrɛ̀	bìsà
	'go!'	'point out!'	'ask!'
(169)	kɔ̀ hɔ́	kyèrɛ̀ nò	bìsà nò
	'go there'	'teach him'	'ask him'
(170)	ɔkɔ̀ (Ak.Fa.)	ɔkyèrɛ́	òbìsá (Ak.As)
	ɔkɔ́ (As)	'he points out'	òbísà (Fa)
	'he goes'		'he asks'
(171)	ɔbékɔ́	ɔbélkyérɛ́	Ak.As: obébíIsá
	'he'll go'	'he'll teach'	Fa : òbébísá / òbebísà
			'he'll ask'
(172)	ɔbékɔ́ hɔ́	ɔbélkyérɛ́ nó	obébísà nò
	'he'll go there'	'he'll teach him'	'he'll ask him'

B   The Noun

The noun in Akan is made up of a stem, usually monosyllabic or disyllabic, and an optional prefix and an optional suffix. Nominal affixes are discussed in detail in Chapter 4. Except in possessive constructions, (pages 69 to 74) and in compounds (pages 74 to 75, and Chapter 5), nouns retain their basic tone patterns in longer constructions. The nouns discussed below may be basic nominal stems or nominalised from verb stems.

1. Monosyllabic nominal stems

Except in very few cases, e.g. àgò 'velvet', monosyllabic noun stems are said on High tone.

àdé (ɛ́)	'thing'	ḿpá	'bed'
ɛwó(ɔ́)	'honey'	àdwé	'kernel'
òsú / èsú	'crying'	àwó(ɔ́)	'child-bearing'

2. Disyllabic nominal stems

a). As explained in Chapter 4, there are some disyllabic stems which are basically monosyllabic. Such nouns have High tone on both syllables.

ɔhéné	'chief'	béré / bérɛ́	'time'
òkúnú	'husband'	ɔsóró	'the skies'
ɔsóḿ	'service'		

b) Basic disyllabic nominal stems usually have High tone on the second syllable, and the favourite tone pattern is Low-High.

ǹtàmá / ǹtòmá	'cloth'	sìká	'gold / money'
ònùá	'sibling'	àtwèré(ɛ́)	'ladder'
òhìá	'poverty'	àwàré(ɛ́)	'marriage'

c) Many disyllabic nominal stems have High-Downstepped High tone pattern.

àdá!ká	'box'	èwú!rá	'rubbish'
ɔkɔ́!tɔ́	'crab'	ɔhɔ́!hó(ɔ́)	'guest / stranger'
pé!né	'agreement'	ká!sá	'speech / language

d) There are a few High-High disyllabic nominal stems.

àdwúmá	'work'	pápá	'good'

e) There are a few disyllabic stems that have a final Low tone, as the following Low-Low stems.

ádàsà	'mankind'	kètè	'a traditional dance'
wɔ̀fà	'uncle'	pàpà	'fan'

f) Very few nouns have High-Low tone pattern, and many of these are English loan words in which the stressed syllable is said on High tone.

òwúrà	'master'	tíkyà	'teacher'
fótò	'photo'	létà	'letter'

C Adjectives and Adverbs

Adjectives and adverbs in Akan are consonant-initial and have no affixes.

Adjectives :	kɛ̀sé	'big'	fɛ̀fɛ́	'beautiful'
	téńtéń	'tall / long'	tùntùm	'black'
	kɔkɔ́ɔ́	'red'	tìà /tìeltíá	'short'

Adverbs :	tùm̀m̀	'black'	kɔ̀ɔ̀	'red'
	háńń	'brightly'	kóḿḿ	'quietly'

These examples show that Akan adjectives tend to be used in their reduplicated form, and that they do not exhibit any regular tone patterns. Adverbs usually are said on monotone - either High or Low tone on all syllables.

CHAPTER 4

THE STRUCTURE OF ʌKAN WORDS

I INTRODUCTION

The structure of words is stated in terms of

A. the stem(s)/ root(s) and affixes that make up the words;
B. the syllable structure of the words.

A Stems and Affixes

Each Akan word is made up of a stem or stems and, in some cases, affixes (prefixes and suffixes) as well. As explained in Chapter 1, the vowels of each Akan word are subject to the rules of Akan Vowel Harmony.

	Prefix(es)	Stem(s)	Suffix	
ofi/efie	o / e	fi	e	'home'
nsu/ensuo	n / en	su	o	'water'
sika	-	sika	-	'money'
anuanom	a	nua	nom	'siblings'
fa	-	fa	-	'take it'
ɔrebɛfa	ɔ, re, bɛ	fa	-	'he's about to take it'
ɔkɔfae	ɔ, kɔ	fa	e	'he went and took it'
odidi	o	di, di	-	'he eats (a lot)'
adidie	a	di, di	e	'eating'
tenten	-	ten, ten	-	'tall / long'
aniɛden	a	ani, yɛ, den	-	'haughtiness'

1. Stems

As can be seen from the examples above a word in Akan may have one or more stems. Two types of stems are distinguished according to how many there are in the word.

    a) Simple (one stem)
    b) Compound (more than one stem)

a) Simple stems
    These are dicussed in Section V below.

b) Compounds
    When two or more stems occur in a word, they may be
i)   different stems, as in the last example above; or
ii)   a repetition of the same stem as in adidie 'eating', where di is
repeated.
    This latter type of compound is referred to as a reduplicated form.
Compounds, including reduplicated forms, are discussed in detail in
Chapter 5.

2. Affixes

    There are two main types of affixes in Akan
a)   Prefixes (these occur before the stem)
b)   Suffixes (these occur after the stem)

    A few compounds have a vowel affix that occurs between the two
stems of the compound in

    i) names of the days of the week in Asante

As: Kwasiada   'Sunday'   *compare* Ak. Fa : Kwasida

    ɛdwoada   'Monday'   Dwowda

    ii) compounds like aniɛden / anuɔden 'haughtiness' ahoɔfɛ
'beauty' may be said to have an affix ɛ / ɔ between the first and last stems
of the compound. This vowel is however analysable as the copula verb
yɛ 'to be' which is reduced to a vowel that takes the lip-position of the
preceding vowel.
    In the discussion on affixes in the next two sections, nothing more is
said of affixes that occur between stems.

B   Syllable Structure

As stated in Chapter 3, the following syllable types occur in Akan.

1. V   :   o / e in o-fi, e-fi-e   'house'

            ɔ   in ɔ-ba   'he comes'

2. CV :   ba   'come'

            ti   in ti-e   'listen'

3. C   :   n   in n-su(o)   'water'

            m   in so-m   'hold it'

            r   in o-fi-r   'he buys on credit' (Fa)

            n /ŋ in ɔ-da-n / ŋ   'he turns (it) over'

Again it was stated in Chapter 3 that tone is also a basic unit of the syllable. In the discussion that follows, however, tone is only mentioned where it is of particular relevance to the point being made.

On the basis of the number of syllables that occur in a word, it may be

a) monosyllabic, that is, with one syllable only

    kɔ   'go'   pa   'good'

b) disyllabic, that is, with two syllables

    tie   'listen'   kɛtɛ   'mat'

c) trisyllabic, that is, with three syllables (also sometimes referred to as polysyllabic)

    hohoro   'wash up'   adaka   'box'

d) polysyllabic, that is, with three or more syllables

    bisebisa   'keep asking'   asɛmpatrɛw   'evangelism'

II NOMINAL AFFIXES

A Nominal Prefixes

A nominal prefix in Akan is either a vowel, a syllabic nasal consonant that has the same place of articulation as the following consonant, or both. Nominal prefixes are said on Low tone, except in very few cases.

	ɔ̀-héné	'chief'	ǹ-tàmá	'cloth'
	à-bá	'seed'	m̀-pá	'bed'
but	á-dàsà	'mankind'	ɛ́bàń / ɛ́m̀àné	'herring'
	álkó	'parrot'		

1. The vowel prefixes, which agree in vowel harmony with the vowel of the stem, are the mid and low vowels **e ɛ a o ɔ**. In Fante the high front vowels **i ẹ** also occur as nominal prefixes.

e-ti(re) / i-tsir	'head'	n-su(o)	'water'
ɛ-wo(ɔ) / e-wo	'honey'	ŋ-kwan	'soup'
a-daka	'box'	m-paboa	'shoes'
o-hia / i-hia	'poverty'	ɔ-hen(e) / e-hen	'chief'

2. In the Asante dialect, nouns that begin with a nasal consonant are often pronounced with a vowel prefixed to the nasal in the citation forms (i.e. when pronounced in isolation), or in emphatic speech.

en-suo	'water'	ɛŋ-kwan	'soup'
ɛm-paboa	'shoes'	en-kyia	'greeting'

3. There are a few words in which the prefix **a** is a followed by a nasal consonant.

am-pesi	'boiled yam / plantain' (Ak.Fa.)
aŋ-kaa / aŋ-kama	'lime'/'orange'(As)

4. Nouns with the prefixes **e ɛ ɔ o** and **i ẹ** (Fa.) are always singular, and often, though not always, have **a** as the prefix in the plural.

Singular nouns that have **a** as the prefix have a nasal prefix in the plural.
Plural nouns may also have the plural suffix in addition to the plural prefix.

ɔhene / ehen	: ahemfo	'chiefs'
ɔpanyin	: mpanyimfo(ɔ)	'elders'
ofi /efie / ifie	: afi(e)	'homes'
aboa	: mboa	'animals'

5. All these prefixes may function as nominalising affixes.

hia	'to need'	ohia / ihia	'poverty'
ko	'to fight'	ɔko	'battle'
dɔm	'to team up'	ɛdɔm / edɔm	'crowd /army'
kɛse	'big'	ɔkɛseɛ	'an important person'
kyia	'to greet'	nkyia	'greeting'

B   Nominal Suffixes

1. Suffix - i /- ẹ

There is a nominalising suffix -i /-ẹ (Ak.Fa.) -iɛ /-ẹɛ (As) that occurs
with some verb stems.

wie	'finish'	awiei / awiɛeɛ	'the end'
tɔ	'to fall'	atɔe / atɔeɛ	'west'
sum	'to lean on'	sumii / sumiɛ	'pillow

2. Asante Nominal Suffix

In the Asante dialect, a mid vowel suffix **e ɛ o ɔ** occurs if the
nominal stem ends in an oral high vowel. The vowel suffix agrees in both
tongue root and lip position with the vowel of the stem.

esi- e	'anthill'	owu- o	'death'
ade- ɛ	'thing'	ɛwo- ɔ	'honey'

83

If the stem ends in a nasalised high vowel, the suffix is the same as the vowel of the stem. This nasalised suffix is however not represented in the orthography.

ɛsẽ̄ -ẽ̄	'teeth'		ɛkɔ̃̄ -ɔ̃̄		'battle'
efĩ̄ -ĩ̄	'dirt'		ehũ̄ -ũ̄		'fear'

Asante noun stems that end in non-high vowels do not have a suffix.

asɔ	'hoe'		ɛka	'debt'
abɛ	'palm tree'		ɛkã̄	'gutter'

3. Plural suffix -fʊ̣ (Ak.Fa), -fʊ̣(ɔ) (As)

This suffix usually occurs with a plural prefix

ɔpanyin	:	mpanyimfo(ɔ)	'elders'
ɔhene	:	ahemfo	'chiefs'
osikani	:	asikafo(ɔ)	'rich people'

4. -fo (Ak.Fa) -foɔ (As) agentive suffix

kua	'farming'		okuafo(ɔ)	'farmer'
boa	'to help'		ɔboafo(ɔ)	'helper'

5. The suffix -ni

This suffix is derived from the noun oni 'person'. The advanced vowel in the suffix assimilates the vowel in the preceding syllable to an advanced quality, as happens in vowel harmony across word boundaries.

Latɛ	'Larteh town'	**Lateni**	'a citizen of Larteh'
sika	'money'	**osikạni**	'a rich person'

6. -wa / -ba Diminutive / Feminine suffix

kuro(w)	town'	kurowa / akuraa	'village'
ᴣsɛɛ	'father' (As)	sewaa	'paternal aunt'
dɔn	'bell'	adɔmba	'(small) bell' (Fa)

7. -nɔm Plural suffix

This is usually suffixed to kinship nouns

agya	'father'	agyanom	'fathers/elders'
yere	'wife'	yerenom	'wives'
nua	'sibling'	anuanom	'siblings'

It also pluralises the word hena / woana / hwae 'who?': henanom woananom / hwaenom

8. Fante and Asante Nominal suffix

As explained in Chapter 3, nouns with High-Downstepped High tone pattern in Asante and Fante have a High tone vowel suffix when they occur as the second element in a possessive noun phrase.

àdáꜜká	:	Kòfí nˊádàkàéˊ / Kòfí ádákàá	'Kofi's box'
ɔhɔꜜhó	:	mé hɔ̀hòéˊ / mè hɔ́hòɔ́	'my guest'

When the noun is an inalienable noun the suffix does not occur.

ènúꜜfú(ɔ́)	:	nˊénùfù / nè núfù	'her breasts'

In Asante, kinship and inalienable nouns, whatever the tone pattern, also lose their suffix when they occur as the second element of the possessive noun phrase, as illustrated by the following examples.

ὲsέέ	:	K̀ofí !sé	'Kofi's father'
àníí	:	K̀ofí ání	'Kofi's eyes'
but àfúó	:	K̀ofí á!fúó	'Kofi's farm'

III ADJECTIVAL AFFIXES

A Prefixes a-, n-

Adjectives do not have prefixes in the singular, but they inflect for plural, and they have the same plural prefixes as nouns, **a-, n-**. The plural forms are often reduplicated.

Singular	Plural	
kɛse	akɛse/akɛseakɛse	'big'
kete-wa	nketenkete	'small'
papa	apapa	'good'
teaa/teateaa	nteateaa	'slender'

as in	ahemfo akɛseakɛse	'big / important chiefs'
	nneɛma nketenkete	'little things'

B Suffixes

1. Diminuṭive Suffix   -wa / -ba / -a

This is a diminutive suffix which occurs with some adjectives to indicate small size.

kete- wa	'small'
korokoro- wa	'round and small'
teatea-a / tsea-ba	slender'

2. Derivational Suffix -ẹ

A suffix -ẹ (sometimes -ẹɛ [-yɛ] in Asante) is used to derive adjectives from some verb stems. This is more common in Fante than in

86

Akuapem and Asante.

nam kyewee	'fried fish' (Fa)
ɛban howee	'smoked herring' (Fa)
nam porɔwee / porɔeɛ	'rotten fish / meat'
aburo(w) guanee / dwanee	'dried corn'

IV   VERBAL AFFIXES

Verbal affixes, except where indicated, agree in vowel harmony with the vowel(s) of the stem.
There are three types of verbal affixes:

A. Subject-concord prefixes
B. Tense / Aspect affixes
C. The Negative prefix

A   Subject-concord prefixes

There are seven subject-concord prefixes corresponding to the seven personal pronouns in Akuapem and Asante, six in Fante.

Pronoun		Prefix
1st person singular	me	me-
2nd pers. sing.	wo /ɔwo	wo-, ɵ- (Fa)
3rd pers. sing.	ɔno	ɔ-
Impersonal (As. Ak.)	ɛno	ɛ-
1st person plural	yɛn / hɛn	yɛ-
2nd pers. plural	mo / hom	mo-, wɔ- (Fa)
3rd pers. plural	wɔn / hɔn /	wɔ-, yɛ- (As)
	wɔɔnom	

It may be pointed out here that traditional subject and possessive pronouns are subject- and possessive-concord markers which agree with their nouns in number and person, as illustrated by the following sentences.

abofra no ɔyɛ adze (Fa)
'child the he-does well'

baa he ɔlɛ (Bron)
'woman the she-says'

mbofra no hɔn ntar (Fa)
'children the their dresses'

Kofi ne dane (Bron)
'Kofi' his house'

m'agya ne nuabea (Ak)
'my father his sister'

The use of both a noun subject/possessor and a concord-marker in the same noun phrase has been lost in most Akan dialects. Only the Bron dialect is so far known to use both consistently.

In Asante the subject or possessor is always expressed either by a noun or by a pronoun.

In Akuapem the subject is always expressed either by a noun or by a pronominal prefix. The possessor is occasionally expressed by both a noun and a concord-marker, as in the above example.

In Fante the subject is sometimes expressed by both a noun and a concord-marker, as in the above example, and at other times either by a noun or by a pronoun. The possessor is always expressed by both a noun and a concord-marker.

In this text the terms pronoun and concord-marker are used interchangeably.

1. 1st person singular pronominal prefix, me-

This prefix agrees with the vowel of the verb stem in being advanced or unadvanced. In Fante, this is the only pronominal prefix that agrees with the vowel of the verb stem in being rounded or unrounded.

In the Future Affirmative, Perfect Affirmative and Past Negative forms of the verb, only the initial consonant of this prefix is pronounced.

Akuapem	Asante	Fante	
mékɔ̀	mèkɔ́	mókɔ̀	'I go'
mìtúì	mìtùì(ɛ)	mùtúì	'I dug it up'
mídì	mìdí	mídzì	'I eat'
métèẁ	mèté	métsèẁ	'I pluck it'
mékɔ́	mékɔ́	mɔ́kɔ́	'I will go'
màáfà	màfá	màáfà	'I've taken it'

2. 2nd person singular pronominal prefix, wo-, ɛ-/ e̩- (Fa)

The prefix wo- occurs in Akuapem and Asante, and agrees with the vowel of the verb stem in being advanced or unadvanced. Unlike the other pronoun prefixes, the 2nd person pronoun prefixes, both singular and plural, are always said on High tone in Akuapem and Asante. In the Perfect Affirmative and Past Negative forms, only the consonant is pronounced.

In Fante the prefix is ɛ- or e̩- if the vowel of the stem is unadvanced, and i- if it is an advanced vowel. In the Perfect Affirmative and Past Negative forms the pronoun prefix is not pronounced.

Akuapem	Asante	Fante	
wókɔ̀	wókɔ́	ékɔ̀	'you go'
wútúì	wútùì(ɛ)	ìtúì	'you dug it up'
wáfà	wáfá	áfà	'you've taken it'

In the unified Akan orthography, wo- is the form that represents the 2nd person singular concord-marker.

3. 3rd person singular pronominal prefix, ɔ-

In Akuapem and Asante this pronoun is used for animate reference, and ɛ-, the Impersonal prefix, for non-animate reference, except in folk tales where trees and stones etc. are invested with human qualities.

In Fante ɔ- is used for both animate and non-animate reference. The prefix agrees in tongue root position with the vowel of the stem.

In the Perfect Affirmative and Past Negative forms of the verb, the pronominal prefix and the Tense/Aspect prefix sequence ɔa- is pronounced wa-. ɔa is the form used in the unified Akan orthography.

	Akuapem, Asante	Fante	
	ɔ́kɔ̀ / ɔ̀kɔ́	ɔ́kɔ̀	'he / she/(it) goes'
	òtúì / òtùì(ɛ)	òtúì	'he / she dug it up / it was uprooted'
ɔafa	wàáfà /wàfá	wàáfà	'he /she/(it) has taken it'

4. The impersonal prefix, ɛ-.

i) In Akuapem and Asante this prefix is used for non-animate reference, whether the noun is singular or plural. It does not occur in Fante. In the Perfect Affirmative and Past Negative forms of the verb the **ɛa-** sequence of the two prefixes is pronounced **a-**, but the full form **ɛa-** is retained in the unified Akan orthography.

	ɛ̀dà há	'it is lying here'
	èsìsì hɔ́	'they, eg. trees, cups, are standing there'
	ètúì / ètùì(ɛ)	'it was uprooted'
ɛaba	ábà / àbá	'it has come'

ii) In Asante this prefix is also used for animate reference, both singular and plural, in emphatic sentences after the emphatic particle **na**. The **na ɛ-** sequence in such utterances is pronounced **nɛ / ne.**

Kòfí nà ɛ̀kɔ̀èɛ̀	'it is Kofi who went'
ǹkɔ̀dàá nó nà èhúìè	'it is the children who saw it'

The Asante use of this prefix for animate reference in emphatic speech is not written. In Akuapem and Fante the 3rd person pronominal prefixes **ɔ-**(singular), **wɔ-** (plural) are used, and these are the forms represented in the unified Akan orthography.

Koti na ɔkɔe	'it is Kofi who went'
mbofra no na wohui	'it is the children who saw it'

5. 1st person plural pronominal prefix, **yɛ-**

This prefix occurs in all three dialects. In the Perfect Affirmative and Past Negative forms of the verb, only the initial consonant is pronounced, but the full form is retained in the spelling.

	Akuapem, Fante	Asante	
	yɛ́kɔ	yɛ̀kɔ́	'we go'
	yétúì	yètùì(ɛ)	'we dug it up'
yɛafa	yàáfà	yàfá	'we've taken it'

90

6. 2nd person plural pronominal prefix, mo-

This prefix occurs in Akuapem and Asante only, and like the 2nd person singular prefix, it is always said on High tone. In Fante the prefix is the same as for the 3rd person plural, wɔ-. Sometimes the Fante 2nd person plural pronoun hom is used with the verb, in which case it is not a prefix, but functions as a noun. In the unified Akan orthography mo- is the form used to represent the 2nd person plural pronominal prefix.

	Akuapem	Asante	Fante	
	mókɔ́	mókɔ́	wɔ́kɔ̀ / hóm̀ kɔ̀	'you go'
	mútúì	mútùì(ɛ)	wòtúì / hóm̀ túì	'you dug it up'
moafa	móáfà	móáffá	wɔ̀áfà / hóm̀ áfà	'you've taken it'

7. 3rd person plural pronominal prefix, wɔ-

This prefix occurs in Akuapem and Fante. In Asante the prefix is the same as for the 1st person plural yɛ-. Sometimes the Asante 3rd person plural pronoun wɔɔnom is used with the verb, in which case it is not a prefix, but functions as a noun.

In the Perfect Affirmative and Past Negative forms of the verb, only the initial consonant is pronounced, but the full form is represented in the spelling.

	Akuapem, Fante	Asante	—
	wɔ́kɔ̀	yɛ̀kɔ́ / wɔ̀ɔ́nóm̀ kɔ́	'they go'
	wòtúì	yètùì(ɛ) / wɔ̀ɔ́nóm̀ tùì	'they dug up'
wɔafa	wàáfà	yàfá / wɔ̀ɔ́nóm̀ áffá	'they've taken it'

In the unified Akan orthography wɔ- is the form used to represent the 3rd person plural pronominal prefix.

The third person plural form of the verb is used to express what is translated as the passive form in English.

| wowiaa no | 'they robbed him / he was robbed' |
| wɔafa | 'they've taken it / it has been taken' |

B Tense and Aspect affixes

1. Future prefix bɛ-

This prefix occurs in the Simple Future and the Immediate Future forms of the verb, and is said on High tone in Fante. In Akuapem and Asante it is High tone in the Simple Future, and Low tone in the Immediate Future.

In the 1st person singular form of the verb only, the full form of the prefix is not pronounced. In the unified orthography the 1st person singular form is spelt **mbɛ-**.

	Akuapem, Asante	Fante	
	ɔbɛ́kɔ́	ɔbɔ́kɔ́	'he will go'
	òbétú	òbótú	'he'll dig it up'
	ɔbɛ́tɛ́(ẃ)	ɔbɛ́tsɛ́ẃ	'he'll pluck it'
	òbédí	òbédzí	'he will eat it'
	ɔ̀rèbɛ̀kɔ́	ɔ̀ròbɔ̀kɔ́	'he's about to go'
	ɔ̀rèbɛ̀tɛ́(ẃ)	ɔ̀rèbɛ́tsɛ́ẃ	'he's about to pluck it'
mbɛkɔ	mɛ́kɔ́	mɔ́kɔ́	'I will go'

2. Progressive prefix re-

This prefix occurs in the Progressive and Immediate Future forms of the verb. It also occurs in the Negative of the Progressive and Future forms of Akuapem and some subdialects of Fante. It has different pronunciations in the different dialects.

In Akuapem it is pronounced **rɛ** with an unadvanced vowel whether the vowel of the stem is advanced or not.

In Asante it is realised as a lengthening of the vowel of the preceding syllable.

In Fante it harmonises with the vowel of the stem in both tongue root position and lip rounding.

Akuapem	Asante	Fante	
ɔ̀rɛ́kɔ̀	ɔ̀ɔ̀kɔ́	ɔ̀rókɔ̀	'he's going'
ɔ̀rɛ́tù	òòtu	òrútù	'he's digging it up'

ɔrèbìsá	òobìsá	òrìbísà	'he's asking'
Kòfí rékɔ̀	Kòfí ìkɔ́	Kòfí rókɔ̀	'Kofi is going'
ɔrèbɛ̀kɔ́	ɔ̀ɔbɛ̀kɔ́	ɔ̀ròbɔ́kɔ́	'he's about to go'
ɔrèbètú	òobètú	òrùbótú	'he's about to dig it up'
ɔrénkɔ́		ɔrónkɔ́	'he won't go'

3. The Perfect prefix, -a

This prefix occurs in Affirmative Consecutive and Perfect forms, and the Past Negative forms of the verb. In Fante this is the only Tense/Aspect prefix that does not agree with the vowel of the stem in being rounded or unrounded.

	Akuapem	Asante	Fante	
	màabà	màbá	màabà	'I've come'
ɔatu	wàatù	wáltú	wèetù	'he's dug it up'
ɔabisa	wàbísá	wàbísá	wèebísà	'he has asked'
	màmbá	màmbá	màmbá	'I didn't come'
ɔambisa	wàmbìsá	wàmbìsá	wèmbísà	'he didn't ask'
ná ɔabisa	wàbísá	wàbísá	wèebísà	'then he would have asked'

As can be seen from the above examples, this prefix is Low tone in Asante. In Fante it is High tone in the Perfect Affirmative, and Low tone in the Past Negative forms. In Akuapem it is Low tone in the Past Negative forms, but in the Perfect Affirmative forms the tone of the prefix depends on the syllable structure of the verb stem, High tone with a monosyllabic stem, Low tone with a disyllabic stem.

4. The Past suffix -i / -ẹ

This is the only suffix in the verbal forms. It occurs in the Past Affirmative and Perfect Negative forms of the verb. There are two different realisations of this suffix depending on whether or not the verb is followed by an object or a complement.

i) Where the verb is not immediately followed by an object or a complement, a Low tone suffix -ı/ -e which agrees with the vowel of the stem in being advanced or unadvanced occurs after the stem.

In Asante the suffix has two alternative forms, either the high front vowel -ı/-e, or -yɛ, and in each case the suffix is preceded by a long vowel. If the stem ends in a vowel, the long vowel is the same quality as that of the final vowel. Where the stem ends in the bilabial nasal **m**, the vowel that occurs before the suffix is a high rounded vowel. Where the stem ends in **n**, the vowel that occurs before the suffix is a high vowel that agrees with the vowel of the stem in lip position.

Akuapem, Fante	Asante	
ɔtɔ̀è	ɔtɔ̀ɔ̀è / ɔtɔ̀ɔ̀yɛ̀	'he bought it'
òǹtúì / óǹtúì	òǹtúúì / òǹtúúyɛ̀	'he hasn't dug it up'
ɔpámèè	ɔpàmèè / ɔpàmòòyɛ̀	'he sewed it'
ɔkánèè	ɔkànèè / ɔkànèèyɛ̀	'he read it'
ɔtɔ́nèè	ɔtɔ̀nèè / ɔtɔ̀nòòyɛ̀	'he sold it'
ɔsáwèè	ɔsàaè / ɔsàayɛ̀	'he scooped out' (eg. water)

In Asante only, where the verb ends in an advanced mid vowel, that is **e** or **o** , this vowel is replaced by the corresponding unadvanced quality **ɛ** or **ɔ** before the suffix. (See Chapter 1 page 23, 6.)

wie	:	òwìɛ́ɛ̀è / òwìɛ́ɛ̀yɛ̀	'he finished it'
osuro	:	òsùrɔ́ɔ̀è / òsùrɔ́ɔ̀yɛ̀	'he was frightened'
bue	:	òm̀búɛ́ɛ̀è / òm̀búɛ́ɛ̀yɛ̀	'he hasn't opened it'

ii) Where the verb is immediately followed by an object or a complement, the suffix is realised as a lengthening of the final vowel, if the stem ends in a vowel. If the stem ends in a consonant, the suffix does not occur but its tone is carried by the final consonant. The unified Akan orthography represents this by doubling the final consonant letter. In Asante such a stem may also be pronounced with a high vowel after the final consonant. (See Chapter 3 for an explanation of the falling pitch on the final vowel of the Fante forms.)

Akuapem	Asante	Fante	
òhúù nò	òhùù nò	òhû nò	'he saw him'
ɔkɔɔ́ hɔ́	ɔkɔ̀ɔ́ hɔ́	ɔkɔ̂ hɔ́	'he went there'
òǹhúù nò	ǹhúù nò	óǹhû nò	'he hasn't seen him'
ɔpáḿ àdé	ɔpàḿ àdéέ /	ɔpáḿ àdzé	'he sewed something'
	ɔpàmòò àdéέ		

5. The ingressive prefixes

There are two prefixes, **bɛ kɔ**, derived from the verbs ba 'come', kɔ 'go', which occur in some Tense/Aspect forms of the verb to indicate a movement towards or away from the speaker, that is required before the action indicated by the the verb. In Fante these prefixes are said on High tone, except in the Past Affirmative forms of the verb. In Asante and Akuapem they are said on Low tone, except in the Perfect and Affirmative Optative (Imperative II) forms of the verb.

Akuapem, Asante	Fante	
ɔkɔ̀fá	ɔkéfá	'he goes and takes it'
òkòdí	òkédzí	'he goes and eats it'
òkòtúì(ɛ)	òkòtúì	'he went and dug it up'
òǹkótúì(ɛ)	óǹkótúì	'he hasn't gone and dug it up'
ɔ̀àkótú	òékótú	'he's gone and dug it up'
ɔ́ǹkɔ́fá	ɔ́ǹkéfá	'let him go and take it'
ɔ́ḿbéfá	ɔ́ḿbéfá	'let him come and take it'
òbèdí	òbédzí	'he comes and eats it'
ɔ̀àbètú	òébótú	'he's come and dug it up'
òbètúì(ɛ)	òbòtúì	'he came and dug it up'

6. The Optative prefix, n-

This is a High tone syllabic nasal which is homorganic with (i.e. with the same place of articulation as) the following consonant. It occurs in the Optative (Imperative II) forms of the verb, as illustrated by the following examples.

ɔ́ŋkɔ́	'let him go'	mɔ́ḿfá	'you (plural) take it'
Kòfí ŋkɔ́	'let Kofi go'	óŋdí	'let him eat it'

C The Negative prefix, n-

This is a syllabic nasal which is homorganic with (i.e. has the same place of articulation as) the following consonant. It is usually said on Low tone. In the Optative Negative form, the High tone of the Optative prefix is replaced by the Low tone of the Negative prefix.

ɔ̀ŋkɔ́	'he doesn't go'/'let him not go'
wóŋkɔ́ / èŋkɔ́	'you do not go'
èntúì(ɛ) / óntúì	'it isn't uprooted'
ɔ̀m̀bɛ̀fá / ɔ̀m̀bɛ́fá	'he doesn't come & take it'

The Optative Negative is spelt with two nasal prefixes, one for the Optative and one for the Negative.

ɔnkɔ	'let him go'	ɔnnkɔ	'let him not go'

The difference between the Affirmative and Negative forms above is however in the tone of the prefix, not in the duration of the nasal that occurs before the verb stem.

Kòfí ŋkɔ́	'let Kofi go'	Kòfí ǹkɔ́	'don't let Kofi go'

In Fante there are three different forms for the Future Negative.

Akuapem	Asante	Fante	
ɔ́rém̀fá	ɔ́m̀fá	ɔ́m̀fá / ɔ́rém̀fá / ɔ̀ŋkɛ́fá	'he won't take it'
ɔ́réǹhú	óǹhú	óǹhú / órúǹhú / òǹkóhú	'he won't see it'
Kòfí réǹhú	Kòfí ǹhú	Kòfí ǹhú / rúǹhú / ǹkóhú	'Kofi won't see it'

In the unified Akan orthography only the form with the nasal prefix and the stem, as in the Asante form, will represent the Future Negative.

It may be noted here that one Negative form negates the Affirmative of the Habitual, Stative, Progressive, the Indefinite and the Immediate Future.

Affirmative	Negative	
Kòfí dá / dà hɔ́	: Kòfí ǹdá hɔ́	'Kofi does not sleep there'
Kòfí dà hɔ́	: Kòfí ǹdá hɔ́	'Kofi isn't lying down there'
Kòfí rèdà / rédà	: Kòfí ǹdá hɔ́	'Kofi isn't sleeping there'(As.Fa)
Kòfí bédá hɔ́	: Kòfí ǹdá hɔ́	'Kofi won't sleep there' (As.Fa)
Kòfí rèbɛ̀dá hɔ́ /	: Kòfí ǹdá hɔ́	'Kofi is not about to sleep
Kòfí rèbédá hɔ́		there' (As.Fa)

V   THE STRUCTURE OF THE SIMPLE STEM

Akan simple stems are usually made up of one or two syllables, and in a few cases, of three or more syllables. The following stem structures occur in Akan.

1. CV	e.g. kɔ	'go'	a-gya	'father'
2. CVV	tie	'listen'	o-wia	'sun'
3. CVC	saw	'to dance'	a-sɔr	'church' (Fa)
	nom	'to drink'	ɔ-dan	'house'
4. CCV	frɛ	'to call'	ɔ-kra	'soul'
5. CVCV	bisa	'ask'	a-daka	'mat'
6. CVCVC	hyerɛn	'brighten'	n-korɔn	'snoring'
7. CVCCV	sunti	'stumble'	a-nanse	'spider'
8. CVCCVC	monkyem	'to twist'		
9. CCVCCV	brantam	'to barricade'		
10. CVCVCV(C)	patiri(w)	'to slip'		

1. CV Stems

This is the most common stem structure in Akan. All the nine vowels of Akan occur in this structure.

di	'eat'		tu	'dig'
fe̩	'vomit'		ko̩	'to fight'
gye	'receive' (Ak)		dwo	'be cool' (Ak)
pɛ	'look for'		kɔ	'go'
ka	'be left behind'			

The advanced mid vowels **e o** occur in very few CV stems in Akuapem and some subdialects of Fante. In Asante **o** occurs in a few words only, as in the examples below.

ago 'velvet' eno 'mother' ako 'parrot' agoo 'knocking!'

Where Akuapem has **e** as in gye 'receive', Asante has e̩ , and Fante has either **e** as Akuapem or e̩ as in Asante. Where Akuapem has **o** as in dwo 'be cool', Asante has o̩, and Fante has either **o** or e̩ as in dwo / dwe̩.

Nasality in CV stems

As far as nasality in CV stems is concerned, where the initial consonant is voiceless, the vowel of the CV stem may be oral or nasalised, but if the consonant is voiced, the vowel is oral, if it is a non-nasal consonant, and nasalised if it is a nasal consonant.

	kã	'say'	ka	'be left behind'
	hũ	'see'	hu	'blow air' (As)
	kyĩ	'squeeze'	kyi	'dislike'
	tõ̩	'bake'	to̩	'throw' (As)
but	mã	'give'	ba	'come'
	nũ	'stir'	du	'arrive'
	nyã	'obtain'	gya	'leave behind '(As)

98

The voiced consonants of Akan are the nasals, the voiced plosives, voiced affricates and the semivowels. It has already been noted in Chapter 2 that semivowels always occur with oral vowels. The distinction between oral and nasalised vowels after voiced consonants is retained in Akuapem and Asante negative forms where the voiced plosive or affricate is assimilated into a nasal consonant.

ba	:	ɔmma	'he doesn't come'
di	:	onni	'he doesn't eat'
gya	:	onnya	'he doesn't leave behind'

compare

mã	:	ɔmmã	'he doesn't give'
nĩ	:	onnĩ	'he doesn't have'
nyã	:	onnyã	'he doesn't obtain'

(**Note**: There are two words, adãã 'deceit' (As), and bãã 'Baah', a name, in which nasalised vowels occur after voiced plosives. These words do not, however, invalidate the point made about the distribution of oral and nasalised vowels after voiced nasal and non-nasal consonants.)

The distribution of oral and nasalised vowels in CV stems makes it possible for the voiced non-nasal consonants and the nasal consonants to be considered as being complementary to each other. In other words **b** is replaced by **m** before nasalised vowels, **d** by **n**, **gy** by **ny**, **dw** by **nw** and so on. This means that the nasals **m, n, ny, nw**, are only variants of **b, d, gy, dw**, respectively before nasalised vowels.

In some cases **ny** and **nw** replace **y** and **ɥ** before nasalised vowels which derive their nasality from a following nasal consonant.

nyãm (Fa)	**yam** (Ak.As)	'grind'
nwɛ̃n (Fa)	**wɛn** (Ak.As)	'watch'

There are words in which these nasals and the voiced oral consonants do contrast before nasalised vowels, but these are CVC stems in which the final consonant is a nasal, and the vowel is a high vowel. In Akan high vowels are nasalised before nasal consonants, so that the nasality of the vowels in the words on the left below is due to the influence of the final nasal consonant. (See Chapter 6, nasalisation of vowels, for a fuller discussion.)

	bḛn	'be cooked'		mḛn	'to swallow'
	dūm	'extinguish'		nūm	'suck'
	dīn	'name'		nĭ̃m	'know'
but	dam	'madness'		nãm	'walk'
	gyam	'mourn with'		nyām	'to wave'

2. CVV Stems

These are disyllabic (two syllables) stems with two vowels which may be identical or different, and which may be both oral or both nasalised. The point made about nasalised vowels and initial voiceless or voiced consonants in CV stems is true of these stems.

	kyea	'bend'		kyḛ̃ã	'walk stylishly'
	toa	'bottle'		tõã	'report'
but	boa	'help'		mõã	'gather'
	daa	'deceive'		nwīĩ	'grumble'

These stems are made up of two syllables for the following reasons.

a) They behave tonally and morphologically (i.e. in word formation) like CVCV disyllabic stems, as can be seen from the following examples where the CVV stem tie 'listen' is compared tonally and in reduplication with a monosyllabic CV stem ka 'say', and with a disyllabic CVCV stem soma 'send on errand'.

Imperative	ká	tìè	sòmà
Habitual	ɔ́kà / ɔ̀ká	òtìé	ɔ̀sòmá
Past	ɔ̀káè / ɔ̀kàè	òtìéì	ɔ̀sòmáè
Future	ɔ̀bɛká	òbéltíé /	ɔ̀bɛ́lsómá
		òbétsèì	
Reduplicated form	kèká	tìétìè	sòmásòmà

In the above examples tie has the same tone patterns as the

disyllabic CVCV stem, and this is true of all CVV stems. The stem tie also reduplicates like a disyllabic CVCV stem, the reduplicated form being a repetition of the consonant and vowels of the stem, unlike the monosyllabic CV stem where the first syllable in the reduplicated form does not repeat the vowel of the stem.

b)   Very often the two vowels are pronounced separately, with a **y** or **w** glide between them where the first vowel is a high front or a high back vowel respectively.

sie	[siye]	'hide'		bua	[buwa]	'cover'
tɛɛ	[tẽyɛ̃]	'straighten'(Ak)		soa	[sọwa]	'carry'

It may be noted here that many CVV stems in Akan correspond to CVCV stems in Nzema, Sehwi and Aowin, which are closely related to Akan.

Akan	Nzema /Sehwi /Aowin	
kae	kakye	'remember'
sɛɛ	sɛke /sɛkye	'spoil'
bue	buke /bukye	'open'
soɛ	sokwɛ	'put down a load'

The two vowels in the CVV stem may be a sequence of

i)   two identical vowels :

	mẹẹ	'eat enough'
	a-poo	'cheating'

Such stems are often used in their reduplicated forms, and in the examples below the simple CVV stems are never used.

daadaa	'deceive'	nwiinwii	'grumble'
poopoo	'bully'	fẹẹfẹẹ	'scrutinise'

ii)   a high vowel followed by a non-high vowel

sie	'hide'	tɛɛ	'straighten' (Ak)

a-bǫa	'animal'	**sua**	'learn'

Some of these CVV stems have a labialised initial consonant

sua [sч̄ā]	'learn'	**bue [bwei / bчie]** 'open'

The different pronunciations associated with such stems are discussed in detail in Chapter 3, under labialisation of consonants.

iii)   a non-high vowel followed by a high front vowel. The vowels in these stems are always oral.

sɛe	'destroy'	**kae**	'remember'
tsei	'listen' (Fa)	**gyae**	'stop'

In some subdialects of Fante such words are often pronounced with a long vowel of the same quality as the first vowel in the sequence.

sɛɛ	'destroy'	**kaa**	'remember'

3.   CVC Stems

The final consonant in these stems may be

m :	nom	'drink'	n / ŋ :	dan / daŋ	'turn over' (Fa.Ak)
r :	sɔr	'get up' (Fa)	w :	kyɛw	'hat' (Ak.Fa.)

These are disyllabic, CV–C, which are analysed as reduced forms of CVCV stems below.

4.   CCV Stems

The second C in these stems is always **r**.

pra	'sweep'	frɛ	'call'

These stems are also disyllabic, and are reduced forms of CVCV stems, as explained in (5) below.

5.   CVCV Stems

There are two main types of such stems

(I)   Those in which the second consonant is a sonorant, that is **r, n, m, w.** These account for the majority of CVCV stems.

(II)   Those in which the second consonant is not a sonorant.

(I)   CVSV stems, that is, those in which the second consonant is a sonorant.

a)   CVrV stems, i.e. where the second consonant is **r.**

All CVrV stems have oral vowels in both syllables. There is one verb **trã** 'sit', which alternates with **tẽnã**, in which a nasalised vowel occurs in a CVrV stem. There are two types of CVrV stems

(1) Where the first vowel is a high vowel, i.e. CIrV, where I stands for a high vowel.

i.   In Akuapem and Asante, where the first vowel is a high front vowel this vowel is only pronounced in slow and deliberate speech, in other words, it is deleted in normal speech, and this pronunciation is reflected in the spelling of some of these words, e.g. **pra** 'sweep'.

kyerɛ / kyrɛ	'show'	**firi / fri**	'buy on credit'
pera / pra	'sweep'	**bere / bre**	'be.red'

As explained in Chapter 3, (page 48) **r** in these words carries the tone of the deleted vowel.

ɔkyr̀ɛ́	'he shows'	**ɔfìrîì**	'he bought on credit'

Where the first vowel is advanced, that is **i**, the initial consonant is palatalised when the vowel is not pronounced.

pira [pyra]	'injure'	**bIrI [byrI]**	'be black'

ii. In Akuapem and Asante, if the first vowel is a high back vowel this vowel is often not be pronounced in normal non-deliberate speech, but the initial consonant is labialised, the labialisation being more pronounced where the high back vowel is advanced, that is **u**. The initial consonant in **kura** below has a further forward articulation on the palate than the initial consonant of **kora**,on account of the advanced tongue position of the following vowel. **h** in **huru** also has the tongue in the position for **u** during its articulation. In the examples below the difference in the tongue position for the initial labialised consonants is indicated by **u** after the labialised consonants with advanced tongue root position.

| kora [kwra] | 'store' | kura [kwura] | 'hold' |
| horo [hwrǫ] | 'wash' | huru [hwuru] | 'jump' |

iii. In Fante the high vowel in the first syllable is deleted in normal non-deliberate speech if the second syllable has a non-high vowel.

| kyerɛ / kyrɛ | 'show' | pra | 'sweep' |

If the second vowel is also a high vowel, this vowel is not pronounced in Fante, and such words end in a final **r**.

| hor | 'wash' | fir | 'buy on credit' |
| sɔr | 'get up' | hur | 'boil' |

As shown in Chapter 3, (page 54) final **r** in these words carries the tone of the deleted final vowel.

| òfir̀ | 'he buys on credit' | ɔkyɛ́r̀ hɔ́ | 'he kept long there' |

(2) Where the second vowel is a high vowel, i.e. CVrI

ˊ i. Where the second vowel is a high vowel, this vowel is not pronounced in Fante, as illustrated by the examples above, and the final **r** is followed by a glottal stop when the stem occurs before pause, as explained in Chapter 2, page 49.

ii. In Akuapem and Asante some of these stems have alternative CV forms in which the second syllable is not pronounced. Both the CVrI and the CV forms are used as free variants in these dialects. The CV forms are said with a final glottal stop when they are followed by pause.

firi / fi	'go out'	kyɛre / kyɛ	'delay'
huru / hu	'boil'	ware / wa	'be long'
kyere / kye	'catch'	dɔre / dɔ	'be fat'

compare

| ware | 'marry' | firi / fri | 'buy on credit' |

The CVrl stems that have the alternative CV forms have a final Low tone syllable, and are either Low-Low or High-Low in tone pattern. They are basically monosyllabic, that is they behave tonally and in other ways (e.g. morphologically, such as in reduplication) like monosyllabic CV stems.

The CVrl stems that do not have alternative CV forms have a basic Low- High tone pattern and are basically disyllabic. This means that they behave tonally and morphologically like disyllabic stems, as illustrated by the following examples. In this book the two types of stems are referred to as Type 1 and Type 2 respectively.

Type 1		Type 2	
kyέrέ	'delay!'	fὲrὲ	'be shy!'
ɔkyέrέ / ɔkyὲr(è)	'he delays'	ɔfὲrέ / ɔfὲr´	'he is shy'
òfîì / òfírîì / òfîì	'he went out'	òfrîì	'he bought on credit'
kyὲkyέ(rέ)		fὲréfὲrὲ	(redup. forms)

compare

hwέ	'look!'	gyìnà	'stop /stand!'
ɔhwέ / ɔhwὲ	'he looks at'	ògyìná	'he stops'
hwὲhwέ		gyìnégyìnà	(redup. forms)

b) Other CVSV stems : CVnV, CVmV, CVwV

(1) Where the second vowel is a high vowel, i.e. CVSI

Like CVrV stems there are two types of these stems: those that are basically monosyllabic, Type 1, and those that are basically disyllabic, Type 2. There are stems in which the second vowel is a high vowel, and like CVrI stems, the final vowel is not pronounced in Fante. The following are examples of Type 1 and Type 2 CVnI and CVmI stems.

Type1			Type 2	
ɔkàṅ / ɔkáṅ		'he reads'	ɔdànè / ɔdáṅ	'he turns over'
ɔsómèè / ɔsòmèè		'he served'	ɔhómèè	'he breathed'

reduplicated forms

kenkan		danedane / dandan
sonsom		homehome

Below are examples of the different pronunciations associated with CVnV, CVmV and CVwV stems. As was stated in the section on the glottal stop in Chapter 1, page 49, the glottal stop occurs after these stems when the final vowel or the final syllable of the stem is not pronounced, and the stem is followed by pause.

	Akuapem	Asante	Fante	
(1)	dɔw	dɔ	dɔw	'weed'
(2)	kaw	ka	kaw	'debt'
(3)	kũm / kũ	kũm / kũ	kũm / kũ	'kill'
(4)	nĩm	nĩmũ / nĩm / nĩ	nyĩm	'know'
(5)	pam	pam	pãm	'sew'
(6)	pam	pamɔ̃ / pam	-	'chase'
(7)	fɛm	fɛm	fɛ̃m	'buy on credit'
(8)	hɔ̃mɛ̃	hɔ̃mɛ̃	hɔ̃m	'breathe'
(9)	hũ	hũnũ / hũ	hũ	'see'
(10)	pɛ̃nɛ̃	pɛ̃nɛ̃	pɛ̃n	'agree'
(11)	daŋ	dany	dãn	'house'
(12)	daŋ	danɛ̃	dãn	'turn over'
(13)	tɔŋ	tɔŋw	tɔ̃n	'sell'
(14)	hɔ̃ŋ	hɔ̃nɔ̃ / hɔ̃ŋw	hɔ̃n	'swell'
(15)	hɔ̃nɔ̃	hɔ̃nɔ̃	hɔ̃n	'dissolve'

The different pronunciations associated with these stems may be summed up as follows:

(i)   CVwV stems

Although there are no stems in current use in which a final vowel occurs in a CVwV form, (tawa 'tobacco', aniwa 'eyes', etc. are CV plus the dimunitive suffix -wa), CVw stems behave tonally and morphologically like Type 1 CVSV stems, and that is why they are grouped together with other CVSV stems.

ɔdɔ̀ẃ	'he weeds'	ɔkáwèè	'he bit it'

reduplicated forms

dòdɔ́ẃ		kèkáẃ

Only oral vowels occur in CVw stems. These stems are pronounced with a final **w** in Akuapem and Fante, but are CV in Asante. Final **w** occurs only in the following words in Asante

ɔhaw	'troubles'	Yaw	'name of a boy born on Thursday'
kyɛw	'hat'	(in the expression	mepa wo kyɛw, 'please')

It may be mentioned here that CVw stems correspond to CVCV stems in Nzema, Sehwi and Aowin, which are closely relatɜd to Akan.

Akan	Nzema /Aowin /Sehwi	
kaw	kakɛ / kalɛ / karɛ	'debt'
pɔw	kpɔkɛ / pɔlɛ / pɔlɛ	'knot'
kyɛw	kyɛlɛ	'hat'

(ii) CVml stems, that is where the second vowel is a high vowel.

(a)   A few Type 1 CVml stems have reduced CV forms which are used interchangeably with CVm forms, examples (3), (4) above.

(b)   In Fante CVml stems are pronounced without the final high vowel, and the first vowel is always nasalised, exx. (3) - (5), (7), (8).

(c)   In Akuapem and Asante, the final vowel may or may not be pronounced.

Where the initial consonant is not nasal, the first vowel is oral if it is a non-high vowel, exx. (5) - (7), but nasalised if it is a high vowel, exx. (3), (4), (8).

There are a few stems however, in which the central vowel **a** is nasalised. The initial consonant in each case is voiceless, and these vowels are basically nasalised, that is, they do not derive their nasality from the following nasal consonant.

ɔ-fãm 'type of cake' siam [syãm] 'pull off'

tãm 'undergarment'

(iii) CVnl stems

Only the verb hūnū / hū 'see' has an alternative CV form. The different pronunciations associated with these stems are stated below for Akuapem, Asante and Fante.

In **Akuapem** these stems are pronounced CVn or CVnV. The CVn forms end in a velar nasal, and the vowel is nasalised if it is a high vowel (14), but oral if it is a non-high vowel, and the initial consonant is non-nasal, (11) - (13). Other examples:

bɛŋ	'be near'	tɔŋ	'sell'
ɔkaŋẹ̃ẹ̃	'he read it'	sẹ̃ŋ	'pass'
hɔ̃ŋ	'swell'	hɔ̃nɔ̃	'dissolve'
nwẹ̃ŋ	'be hard'	nwẹ̃nẹ̃	'weave'
mãŋ	'turn aside'	huãnẹ̃	'scratch'

In huãnẹ̃ 'scratch' the non-high vowel is basically a nasalised vowel, in other words it does not derive its nasality from the following consonant. (Stewart, 1976, suggests that the Akuapem stems that have a CVnV pronunciation basically have nasalised vowels, and those with a CVn pronunciation basically have oral vowels, as reflected in pairs of words such as hɔ̃ŋ and hɔ̃nɔ̃ above, and huaŋ 'pull away', huãnẹ̃ 'scratch'. This does not however explain why words like mãŋ 'turn' and nãŋ 'melt' with a nasalised non-high vowel and an initial nasal consonant have a final ŋ instead of nẽ.)

In **Asante** Type 1 CvnV stems may be pronounced with or without the final vowel (14). Other examples:

bɛn	'be near'	mẽn / mẽnẽ	'swallow'
kwan / kwanẽ	'cackle'	kyɛn / kyɛnɛ	'surpass'

108

The final vowel is usually pronounced in Type 2 stems, exx. (10), (12). Other examples:

bɔnē 'evil'   mānē 'send money / food'

Where the stem has a CVn form, it is pronounced with a tongue movement from the vowel sound towards a palatal nasal **ny** or a labialised velar nasal **ŋw** depending on whether the vowel is front or back respectively. This final nasal consonant position may not be reached where the vowel of the stem is a non-high vowel, so that the stem may end in a nasalised high vowel.

kan	: kany / kaę̃	'read'	tɔn	: tɔŋw / tɔǫ̃	'sell'
din	: dĩny	'name'	hon	: hǫ̃ŋw	'swell'
sɛn	: sɛny / sɛę̃	'how much'	ben	: bę̃ny	'be cooked'

The first vowel is nasalised if it is a high vowel, but oral if it is a non-high vowel. Even where the stem ends in a nasalised high vowel, nasality on the non-high vowel is slight, and starts towards the end of the articulation of the non-high vowel.

When a CVn form occurs with the -iɛ /-ę̃ɛ Past or Adjectival suffix, the stem ends in - n.

ɔkanɛɛ	'he read it'	ɔtɔnɛɛ	'he sold it'
epuniɛ	'it was blackened with smoke'	dwanee(ɛ̃)	'dried'

In **Fante** all such stems are pronounced CVn, and like Fante CVm forms the vowels in these stems are always nasalised.

kãn	'read'	tɔ̃n	'sell'
dzĩn	'name'	hǫ̃n	'swell'

In some Fante sub-dialects these stems are pronounced with a tongue movement from the nasalised vowel towards **ny** or **ŋw** depending on whether the vowel is front or back, as in Asante, or with a long nasalised vowel, as in the following examples.

ɔkwãny / ɔkwãã 'road'   tɔ̃ŋw / tɔ̃ɔ̃ 'sell'

dzĩny / dzĩ̄ 'name'   hõŋw / hȭǭ   'swell'

(2) Where the second vowel of the CVSV stem is a non-high vowel

The only non-high vowel that occurs in this position is nasalised **a**.
These stems do not have reduced forms, and the vowels are all
nasalised.

sõmã	'send on errand'	põmã	'walking stick'
gyĩnã	'stand /stop'	mãnã	'send food / money' (Ak)

(II) Other CVCV stems, that is where the second consonant is not a
sonorant.

Such stems always have a CVCV pronunciation in all dialects. Where
the initial consonant is not a nasal, the vowel oi the first syllable is always
oral, and only the vowel of the second syllable may be nasalised. Where
the initial consonant is a nasal, the first vowel is nasalised.

bisa	'ask'	fitĩ̄	'pierce'
kita / kuta	'hold'	kusã / kisã	'turn over'
nũfu	'breast'.	nĩ̄ã	'right hand side'
pagya	'lift'	hodwo	'slacken'

6. Other stem structures

The five stem structures CV, CVV, CVC, CCV, CVCV, discussed above
are the basic simple stem structures of Akan, and account for the majority
of Akan stems. Simple stems of larger structure may be described in
terms of a combination of two of these structures.

a-nanʊ̀ɕ	:	CVC*-CV	'spider'
hyerɛn	:	CV-CVC	'brighten'
a- pɔtorɔ	:	CV-CVCV	'frog' (Ak)
monkyem	:	CVC*-CVC	'twist'

* The second consonant in the CVC structure is always a nasal which has
the same place of articulation as the following consonant.

IV THE TONE OF THE VERB STEM

As discussed in Chapter 3, the verb in Akan has different tone patterns depending on factors such as the Tense or Aspect of the verb and the basic tone pattern of the stem. What follows is a statement of the basic tone patterns of monosyllabic and disyllabic verb stems. The tones of other stems - nouns, adjectives and adverbs - have already been discussed in Chapter 3.

A Monosyllabic CV stems

1. High tone CV stems

There are CV verb stems which are basically High tone, as reflected in the following examples.

yɛ́	'do it'	kɔ́	'go'
ɔyɛ́è	'he did it' (Ak.Fa)	ɔkɔ́è	'he went' (Ak.Fa)
ɔbéyɛ́	'he'll do it'	ɔbékɔ́	'he'll go'
ɔ̀nyɛ́	'he doesn't do it'	ɔ̀nkɔ́	'he doesn't go'

However these stems are not always said on High tone in all the Tense and Aspect forms of the verb, that is, the basic tone of the verb stem may change depending on the Tense or Aspect (and sometimes the dialect) in which it occurs.

Ak.Fa :	ɔ́yɛ̀	'he does it'	As.	:	ɔyɛ́
As. :	ɔyɛ̀è	'he did it'	Ak.Fa :	ɔyɛ́è
Ak.Fa :	ɔréyɛ̀	'he's doing it'	As.	:	ɔrèyɛ́

2. Low tone CV stems

i) There are CV stems that are basically Low tone, and this Low tone is regularly reflected only in Asante Progressive Affirmative and Past Negative forms of the verb, as illustrated by the following examples.

ɔrèfà	'he's taking it'	ɔrègyà	'he's receiving it'
ɔrèpɛ̀	'he's looking for it'	ɔrètwà	'he's cutting it'

màńdà	'I didn't sleep'	màngyè	'I didn't receive it'

compare Asante High tone stems

ɔrèbá	'he's coming'	ɔrèyɛ́	'he's doing it'
màmbá	'I didn't come'	màntɔ́	'I didn't buy it'

Fante Future forms also reflect the basic Low tone of such CV stems, although in some subdialects the stem is also said on High tone and the two pronunciations are used interchangeably.

ɔbɛ́fà / ɔbɛ́fá	'he'll take'	ɔbégyè / ɔbégyé	'he'll receive'
ɔbɛ́pè / ɔbɛ́pɛ́	'he'll look for it'	obótwà / obótwá	'he'll cut it'

compare Fante High tone stems

ɔbɛ́yɛ́	'he'll do it'	ɔbɔ́tɔ́	'he'll buy it'

In Asante the contrast between a High tone stem and a Low tone stem is sometimes carried, not by the verb, but by the pronoun object that follows it.

Low tone stem		High tone stem	
ɔbégyé nò	'he'll receive him'	ɔbɛ́yɛ́ nó	'he'll insult him'
èbétwá mè	'it will cut me'	ɛbékɔ́ mé	'it will fit me'

Akuapem CV verb stems do not reflect this contrast between High tone and Low tone stems.

Low tone stem		High tone stem	
ɔrétwà	'he's cutting it'	ɔrétɔ	'he's buying it'
ɔbɛ́fá	'he'll take it'	ɔbébá	'he'll come'
obégyé mé	'he'll receive me'	ɛbékɔ́ mé	'it will fit me'

ii) A few Low tone CV stems occur only in the Stative form of the verb.

so :	ɔsò àdé(ɛ)	'he has a load on his head'
te :	ɔtè hɔ́	'he lives there / is seated there'
wɔ :	mèwɔ̀ bì	'I have some'

There are other stems with similar meaning which occur in the other Tense/ Aspect forms of the verb.

so	:	soa	-	ɔsɔ́á ádé(ɛ)	'he carries something'
te	:	tena	-	ɔbéłténá hɔ́	'he'll live /sit there'
wɔ	:	nya	-	màǹyá bì	'I've obtained some'

B   Disyllabic stems

The disyllabic stem structures that occur are

1. Type 1 CVS(V)
2. Type 2 CVS(V)
3. Other CVSV
4. CCV
5. CVV
6. Other CVC\

Tonally these fall into three groups

1.   Tone group I

This group is made up of Type 1 CVS(V) stems, and they are tonally like monosyllabic stems. The second syllable is Low tone, but the first syllable may be High tone or Low tone, so that these stems may have a basic High-Low or Low-Low tone pattern. Like Low tone CV stems, the tone of stems with basic Low-Low tone pattern is reflected regularly only in Asante Progressive Affirmative and Past Negative forms.

ɔ̀rèkyɛ̀(rè)   'he's keeping long'   ɔ̀rèsòm   'he's serving'

compare High-Low stems

ɔ̀rèhóró   'he is washing it'   ɔ̀rènóm   'he is drinking'

Like Low tone CV stems, there are Low-Low Type 1 CVC(V) stems that occur only in the Stative form of the verb, and are replaced by other stems with similar meaning in the other Tense /Aspect forms of the verb.

ɔ̀nàm   'he is walking'   ɔ̀nànté(ẁ)   'he walks'

113

| òmìm | 'he knows' | òbéhú(nú) | 'he'll know /see' |
| ɔ̀nyèm | 'she's pregnant' | ònyìnsɛ́nèè | 'she became pregnant' |

2. Tone group II

This group includes

a) Type 2 CVS(V)
b) Other CVSV
c) CCV
d) CVV

These stems have a basic Low-High tone pattern which is reflected in some Tense/ Aspect forms of the verb.

mèdàń / mèdàné	'I turn over' (Ak.As)
ògyìná	'he stops /stands'
ɔ̀rèsòmá	'he is sending a messenger'
ɔ̀rénkàé / ɔ́nkàé	'he won't remember' (Ak.As)
mèkyèréè	'I showed /pointed it out'(Ak.As)
mèrèbèkòrá	'I'm about to store (it)' (Ak.As)

The Low-High pattern is often reflected in the nominalised forms of these stems.

ɔ̀frɛ́	'call'
àgyìná	'consultation by a few people standing aside'
àsòmá	'habit of sending people on errands'
hòméldá	'holiday/ day of rest'

In Fante only, some of these stems behave tonally like Group III stems below.

3. Tone group III

There are only a few CVCV verb stems in which the second consonant is not a sonorant, that is not **r,n**, or **m**. These also have a basic Low-High tone pattern, as reflected in the following verbs.

114

òbìsá	'he asks' (Ak.As)
ɔ̀rèhàtá	'he's spreading (it) out to dry' (Ak.As.)
ɔ̀kàsáè	'he spoke'
ɔ̀bɛ́pá!gyá	'he will lift it' (Ak.As)

In the last example the Low-High stem occurs after a High tone prefix, resulting in a H-L-H sequence. The Low tone is subsequently replaced by High tone, resulting in the H-H-!H tone pattern, (Chapter 3 page 60).

In Fante these stems generally have a High-Low pattern as reflected in the verbs below.

òbísà	'he asks'
ɔ̀rèhátà	'he's spreading (it) out to dry'
òbébísà	'he will ask'
òrìbébísà	'he's about to ask'

As stated on page114 some Group II verbs in Fante have the same tone patterns as Group III stems.

òtséì	'he listens'
ɔ̀bɛkáè	'he will remember'
òrìtséì	'he is listening'
òrìbétséì	'he's about to listen'
ɔ̀dáǹ	'he turns over'
ɔ̀bɛ́dáǹ	'he will turn over'

Schachter and Fromkin (1968) account for the tone patterns of these Fante Group II verb stems in terms of a lost voiceless second consonant in the CVV forms, and they derive the **n** of stems like dan(e) 'turn over', man(e) 'change direction', from an underlying **k**, which becomes **ŋ** in Akuapem and **n** in Fante. In their analysis these Group III stems have a basic High-Low tone pattern.

In the analysis presented here, both Group II and Group III disyllabic stems have a basic Low-High tone pattern, as illustrated by the following Akuapem and Asante examples.

Group II		Group III	
ògyìná	'he stops'	òbìsá	'he asks'
ɔ̀rèkyèrɛ́	'he is showing'	ɔ̀rèkàsá	'he is speaking'
ɔ̀dànèè	'he turned'	ɔ̀pàtàè	'he pacifed (him)'

The two groups of stems however behave tonally differently in some environments. For example in the Future form of the verb, the H-L-H sequence resulting from the prefixation of the High tone Future prefix to the stem yields, in the Akuapem and Asante dialects, a H!HH pattern with Group II stems but HH!H with Group III stems. In other words High tone spreading to the intervening Low tone is from right to left (i.e. from the stem final High tone syllable) for Group II stems, but from left to right (i.e. from the prefix) for Group III stems.

Group II		Group III	
ɔ̀bélpéné	'he will agree'	ɔ̀békàlsá	'he will speak'
ɔ̀bélkyérɛ́	'he will show'	òbébílsá	'he will ask'
ɔ̀bélbóá	'he will help'	ɔ̀bɛ́pàltá	'he will pacify'

The difference between these two groups of stems is also reflected in some nominalised forms.

àgyìná	'consultation between a few people standing aside'	kálsá	'language'
m̀bòá	'help'	m̀páltá	'pacification'
àsòmá	'sending people on errands'	àbílsá	'consulting juju'
but			
àdèkyèrɛ́	'teaching'	àsèmbìsá	'question'

These last examples, which are compounds, reflect the basic Low-High tone pattern of the two groups of stems.

CHAPTER 5

COMPOUNDS

I   INTRODUCTION

Compounds are made up of two or more stems, as in the examples below.

Compound		Stems	
didi	'eat'	di, di	'eat'
ahimfie	'palace'	ɔ-hene, ǝ-fi-e	'chief', 'home'
asɛmpatrɛw	'evangelism'	a-sɛm, pa, trɛw	'news, good, spread'

The first example, didi, is a reduplicated form, a compound in which the same stem is repeated. This is a frequent form of compound formation in Akan, and is discussed in Section III below.

II   THE PHONOLOGY OF COMPOUNDS

Akan compounds, whether reduplicated or not, undergo certain phonological processes. These are

1. vowel harmony
2. homorganic nasal assimilation
3. loss of final vowel or final syllable
4. loss of vowel or nasal prefix
5. nasalisation of voiced plosives
6. changes in the basic tones of stems

Each compound may undergo one or more of these processes.

1.   Vowel Harmony

As explained in Chapter 1, vowel harmony in Akan is basically a regressive process in which advanced vowels assimilate unadvanced vowels that precede them. This is true of vowel harmony in compounds. In the following examples an advanced vowel **I** or **u** assimilates a preceding unadvanced vowel to an advanced vowel quality.

117

abotire	'headgear'	:	bɔ, eti(re)	'tie', 'head'
asenhunu	'nonsense'	:	asɛm, hunu	'news', 'empty'
dwenini	'ram'	:	odwan, nini	'sheep', 'male'
adisua	'learning'	:	ade, sua	'thing', 'learn'
but in tibɔne	'bad luck'	:	eti(re), bɔne	'head', 'bad'

the vowels in the second part of the compound remain unadvanced because they occur *after* the advanced vowel in eti.

2. Homorganic Nasal Assimilation

In Akan when a nasal consonant occurs in the same word before another consonant, it is homorganic with that consonant, that is, it has the same place of articulation as that consonant. In the following examples, the Negative prefix is homorganic with the initial consonant of the verb stem.

mpam	'don't sew it'
ntu	'don't dig it up'
ɔŋkɔ	'he doesn't go'

Homorganic nasal assimilation refers to the process in which a nasal consonant takes the place of articulation of the consonant adjacent to it, as in the following examples where the final nasal in the first word is replaced in the compound by a nasal that is homorganic with the following consonant.

asendi	'judgement'	:	asɛm, di	'case', 'settle'
kɔmpɔw	'goitre'	:	kɔn, pɔw	'neck', 'knot'
ahimfie	'palace'	:	ɔhene, efie	'chief', 'home'

There are a few exceptions to this process, however, as illustrated by the following examples.

nimde(ɛ)	'knowledge'	:	nim, adeɛ	'know', 'thing'
enyimnyam	'glory' (Fa)	:	enyim, nyam	'face', 'glory'

3. Loss of final vowel or final syllable

It was pointed out in the discussion on CVCV stems that those in which the second consonant is a sonorant - r n m w - sometimes have the final vowel or the final syllable deleted.

hunu / hu	'see'		nim / ni	'know'
firi / fir / fi	'go out'		saw / sa	'dance'
dane / dan	'turn over'		hono / hon	'swell'

The deletion of the final vowel or final syllable also takes place when these stems occur as the first element in a compound.

ahimfie	'palace'	:	ɔhene, efie	'chief', 'home'
tibɔne	'bad luck'	:	etire, bɔne	'head', 'bad'
ayeforo	'bride'	:	ɔyere, (fo)foro	'wife', 'new'
dwenini	'ram'	:	oguan / odwan, nini	'sheep', 'male'

In the last example the final **n** of oguan / odwan is deleted because the following stem begins with a nasal. There are a few exceptions, however, as in enyimnyam 'glory' above.

4. Loss of vowel or nasal prefix

It was pointed out in Chapter 1 that unlike other vowel nominal prefixes, the prefix **a** is not deleted when the noun occurs in a nominal construction. The same is true of the nasal nominal prefix. In compounds however, such prefixes may be deleted if the noun in question is not the first element in the compound.

akɛsesɛm	'big talk'	:	kɛse, asɛm	'big', 'talk'
nimdeɛ	'knowledge'	:	nim, adeɛ	'know', 'thing'
yarepa	'sick bed'	·	ɔyare, mpa	'illness', 'bed'
abɛkwan	'palm soup'	:	abɛ, nkwan	'palmnuts', 'soup'

5. Nasalisation of voiced plosives and affricates

In the Akuapem and Asante dialects, when a voiced plosive or affricate occurs after a nasal consonant in the same word, that plosive is replaced by a nasal consonant, as in the following compounds.

asenni	'judgement'	:	asɛm̩ di	'case', 'settle'
akyinnye	'disbelief'	:	okyim̩ gye	'doubt', 'receive'
asennu	'crucifix'	:	sɛn̩ dua	'hang', 'tree /wood'

As can be seen from the above examples, the homorganic nasal assimilation process takes place before the nasalisation of the voiced plosive or affricate, that is, in asenni for example, the final **m** of asɛm is first replaced by an alveolar nasal n ,on account of the following alveolar consonant in di The voiced alveolar plosive is then assimilated into a nasal.

There are a few exceptions, however, as in **nimdeɛ** 'knowledge'

6. Changes in the basic tones of the stems

The tone patterns of compounds, other than reduplicated forms, are of two main types. These are related to the tone of the first stem in the compound, and there is no evidence that the type of tone pattern a compound has is related to the word classes of the stems from which the compound is derived.

a) Compounds in which all the syllables of the first stem are said on Low tone, irrespective of the basic tone pattern of the stem.
b) Compounds in which the first stem is not said on Low tone.

a) First stem said on Low tone
This is the most common tone pattern for compounds.

i) Noun plus Noun compounds

In this group of compounds, the first noun qualifies the second.

àhìm̀fíé	'palace'	:	ɔ́héné	'chief'	èfíó	'home'
dwènìní	'ram'	:	òdwáń	'sheep'	níní	'male'

nàntwìnáḿ	'beef'	:	nàntwíé	'cow'	ɛnáḿ	'meat'
nìsúó	'tears'	:	àní	'eye'	ǹsúó	'water'
àsàmàmpɔ́ẃ	'burial-grove'	:	ɔsálmáń	'ghost'	pɔ́ẃ	'thicket'

ii) Object plus Verb compounds

In these compounds there is a reversal of the verb-object word order of Akan phrase structure.

àdìsùá	'learning'	:	àdé	'thing'	sùá	'learn'
màǹsòtwé	'litigation'	:	máǹsó	'discord'	twè	'drag'
àkyìǹgyé / àkyìǹnyé	'disbelief'	:	òkyíḿ	'doubt'	gyè	'receive
àsèmmìsá	'question'	:	àsɛḿ	'matter'	bìsá	'ask'
àbùsùabɔ́	'member-ship of a family'	:	àbùsùá	'family'	bɔ́	'make'

iii) Verb plus Object compounds

(1)

m̀mùasóó	'lid'	:	bùá	'cover'	ɛsó	'top'
dìbèá	'rank'	:	dí	'take/have'	bèá	'place'
àbòtíré	'headgear'	:	bɔ́	'tie'	ètíré	'head'
ǹsìhó	'interest'	:	sì	'be fixed'	ɛhó	'exterior'
nìmdeɛ / nyìmdzèé	'knowledge'	:	nìm / nyìm	'know'	àdéɛ / àdzé	'thing'

(2) In the following examples both stems are said on Low tone

àwèǹnàdé	'lion'	:	wé	'chew'	ǹnàdé	'metal'
àgyèmàǹ	'savior'	:	gyè	'rescue'	ɔmáń	'state'
àtètènkr̀ònà	'murderer'	:	tèté	'pluck'	kr̀ònà	'heart'
àdìkàǹfo	'pioneers'	:	dí	'take'	ɛkáń	'first'

| àbùbùmmàbàa | 'type of caterpillar' | : | bùbú | 'break' | m̀màbàá | 'twigs' |

iv) Noun plus Adjective compounds

ɔ̀hèǹkɛ̀sé	'great king'	:	ɔ̀héné	'chief'	kɛ̀sé	'big'
ǹsèǹhúnú	'nonsense'	:	àsɛ́m̀	'talk'	húnú	'empty'
òguàǹtéń	'long-legged sheep'	:	òguáń	'sheep'	téń	'tall'
tìbɔ̀né	'bad luck'	:	ètíré	'head'	bɔ̀né	'bad'
nàmpá	'choice meat / fish'	:	ɛ̀náḿ	'meat / fish'	pá	'good'

v) Adjective plus Noun compound

| àkɛ̀sèsɛ́m̀ | 'big talk' | : | kɛ̀sé | 'big' | àsɛ́m̀ | 'talk' |

b) First stem not said on Low tone

i) Noun plus Noun compounds

̀ɔ̀kókóníní	'cockerel'	:	àkókɔ́	'chicken'	níní	'male'
́ḿpɔ́ẁ	'goitre'	:	ɛ̀kɔ́ń	'neck'	pɔ́ẁ	'knot'
tíń!wí	'hair'	:	ètíré	'head'	ǹwí	'hair'
àsɔ́réldáń	'chapel'	:	àsɔ́ré	'church'	ɔ́dáń	'building'
yàrélpá	'sick bed'	:	ɔ̀yàré	'illness'	m̀pá	'bed'

Although there is no modification in the tone patterns of the two nouns in each of the above compounds, (the Downstepped High tones in the last three examples are due to either an assimilated Low tone or to a lost Low tone) each of these compounds function syntactically as one unit.

ii) Object plus Verb compounds

Like the Object plus verb compounds in (a) (ii) above, the normal

122

verb-object word order of Akan phrase structure is reversed in these compounds.

òsélbɔ́	'jubilation'	:	òsé	'outcry'	bɔ́	'make'
àháályɔ́	'hunting'	:	ɛ̀há	'hunting'	yɛ́/yɔ́	'do'
àbéltwá	'palm-wine making'	:	àbɛ́	'palm tree'	twà	'cut'
ǹtɛ́mlpɛ́	'haste'	:	ǹtɛ́m	'quickly'	pɛ̀	'want'
àkáldán	'debt colletion'	:	káẃ	'debt'	ɗàn	'demand'

The verb, which is the second element in these compounds, is always said on High tone, whether it is a High tone or a Low tone verb. It is not clear why the High tones on the verbs in these compounds are downstepped.

iii) Verb plus Object compounds

The verb stems in these compounds are said on High ton̄ irrespective of their basic tone pattern.

(1)	àyɛ́dé	'object'	:	yɛ́	'do'	àdé	'thing'
	àtúbóá	'a fly'	:	tù	'fly'	àbóá	'animal'
	àsénlnúá	'crucifix'	:	sɛ̀n	'hang'	ɗúá	'tree/wood'
	àbódín	'title'	:	bɔ́	'call'	dín	'name'
(2)	kyɛ́adéɛ́	'generous person'	:	kyɛ́	'share'	àdéɛ́	'thing'
	ɔbɔ̀adéɛ́	'creator'	:	bɔ́	'make'	àdéɛ́	'thing'
	kɔ̀ayíé	'one who goes to funerals regularly'	:	kɔ́	'go'	àyíé	'funerals'
	díàbóró	'malicious person'	:	dí	'use'	àbóró	'malice'

In Asante these compounds have the same tone patterns as when the component words occur in a sentence.

ɔkyɛ́ àdéɛ̀ 'he's generous'   ɔkɔ́ àyíé 'he goes to funerals'
compare Akuapem and Fante

ɔkyɛ̀ àdé   ɔkɔ̀ àví

123

iv) Verb plus Verb compounds

The verb stems in these compounds are said on High tone whatever their basic tone patterns.

gyídí	'faith'	:	gyè	'receive'	dí	'eat'
súfrɛ́	'appeal'	:	sú	'cry'	frɛ́	'call'
ɔkámáfó	'advocate'	:	ká	'speak'	mà	'act on behalf of'
ántɔbórɔ́	'one who gets drunk at other's expense'	:	n̄-tɔ́	'not buy'	bòrò	'be drunk'
nsɔhwɛ́	'tribulations'	:	sɔ́	'try'	hwɛ́	'see'

The verbs in these compounds occur in the order in which they would normally occur in a serial verb construction, as illustrated by the examples below.

| mègyè nó dí | 'I believe in him' |
| sú frɛ̀ nò | 'call on him for help' |

v) Adjective plus noun compound

| àfɛfɛdé | 'beautiful / vain things' | : | fɛfɛ́ | 'beautiful' | àdéɛ́ | 'thing' |

III REDUPLICATED FORMS

Reduplication is a type of compound-formation which consists of the repetition of the whole or part of a stem. Reduplication is a common process of word formation in Akan. Some reduplicated forms are a simple repetition of the stem, as in

pá   'good'   pápá

In this example, the reduplicated form is made up of two parts, each of which is identical to the simple stem in both the consonant and vowel as well as in tone. Most reduplicated forms however have a more complex structure, as shown by the following examples.

124

pá	'skim'	pɛ̀pá / pɔ̀pá
fɛ́ẃ	'thrive'	fɛ̀fɛ́ẃ
fɛ̀ẁ	'beautiful'	fɛ̀fɛ́ (Ak) fɛ̀ɛfɛ́ (As) fɛ̀ɛfɛ́ẃ (Fa)
twàm̀	'wither'	twìntwám̀

A Reduplicated Verbs

(I) Monosyllabic CV stems

(1)	tu	'dig'	tu*tu*
(2)	dwo	'cool down' (Ak)	dwu*dwo*
(3)	gye	'receive' (Ak)	gyi*gye*
(4)	hwɛ	'look at'	hwɛ*hwɛ*
(5)	bɔ	'break'	bɔ*bɔ*
(6)	fɛ̣	'vomit'	fɛ̣*fɛ̣*
(7)	da	'sleep'	dɛ̣*da*
(8)	twa	'cut'	twi*twa*
(9)	pa	'skim surface'	pɛ̣*pa* / pɔ̣*pa*

Each of these reduplicated forms is made up of two parts, a prefix and the stem, which is italicised. The phonological features of these reduplicated forms are as follows:

a) The prefix is CV, like the stem.
b) The initial consonant of the stem is repeated in the prefix.
c) The vowel of the prefix in all the examples is a high vowel i ɛ̣ ɔ̣ u whether the vowel of the stem is high or not.
d) In examples (1) to (6) the vowel of the prefix agrees with the vowel of the stem in two dimensions of vowel harmony
   i) both vowels are either advanced (exx.1 - 3) or unadvanced (exx. 4 - 6)
   ii) both vowels are either back and rounded (exx.1,2,5), or front and unrounded (exx. 3,4,6)
e) Where the vowel of the stem is the open vowel **a**, the vowel of the prefix is
   i) advanced and unrounded if the initial consonant of the stem is a

palatal or a palatalised consonant, (ex. 8).

Other examples :	nya	'become sour'	ny*inya*
	sia	'be suspended'	si*sia*
	gya	'leave behind' (As)	gy*igya*

(As was stated under exceptions to vowel harmony (page 20) syllables made up of a palatal or palatalised consonant followed by **a** have advanced vowels in preceding syllables.)

ii) advanced and rounded if the initial consonant is labial-palatalised, or is any of the labialised consonants which have been described as having an advanced tongue root position, with the back of the tongue raised in the position for **u**, page 21.

	sua	'be small'	su*sua*
	gua	'cut up' (Ak)	gu*gua*
	twa	'cut'	twu*twa* / twi*twa*

In the last example, the two reduplicated forms are used interchangeably, although the one with the unrounded vowel **i**, is the preferred form.

iii) unadvanced if the initial consonant is not any of the palatal, palatalised or labialised consonants referred to above, (exx. 7, 9).

other examples:	fa	'take'	fẹ*fa* / fọ*fa*
	ka	'say'	kẹ*ka*
	kwa	'polish floor' (As)	kọ*kwa*
	pa	'skim surface'	pẹ*pa* / pọ*pa*

iv) As can be seen from the examples, if the initial consonant of the stem is labial, the vowel of the prefix may be rounded or unrounded. The two reduplicated forms occur as free variants, although individual dialects show preference for one form or the other. Where the initial consonant is **kw** the vowel of the prefix is unadvanced and rounded. (Syllables with **kw** and **w** followed by **a** do not have an advanced vowel in the preceding syllable, page 21.)

f) In the reduplicated form of a nasalised CV stem, if the initial consonant is non-nasal, the vowel of the prefix is always oral, and only the

126

second syllable may be nasalised. In this regard, these reduplicated forms are similar to the simple disyllabic stem, as illustrated by the examples below. (See also page 110 (II).)

Verb stem		Redup. form	cf.	Disyllabic stems	
tɔ	'buy'	totɔ		bisa	'ask'
kā	'say'	kekā		kʊsā	'turn over'
tọ̄	'bake'	tọtọ̄		fitī	'pierce'
but mā	'give'	mẹ̄mā		mānā	'send food / money'

(II)   Reduplicated forms of Type 1 CVC(V)

(10)	sɛw	'spread out'	sẹsɛw
(11)	kaw	'bite' (Ak.Fa)	kẹkaw
(12)	dɔw	'weed'	dọdɔw
(13)	fir(i)	'go out'	fifiri / fifir
(14)	dɔr(ẹ)	'be fat'	dọdɔrẹ / dọdɔr
(15)	tɔn	'sell'	tọntɔn
(16)	kan	'read'	kẹŋkan
(17)	mẹn(ẹ)	'swallow'	mẹmẹnẹ / mẹmẹn
(18)	họn(ọ)	'swell'	hoŋhọnọ / hoŋhọn
(19)	dum	'extinguish'	dundum / dunnum
(20)	nam	'walk'	nẹnam
(21)	twam	'wither'	twintwam
(22)	kwan	'wind cloth round'	kọŋkwan
(23)	guan	'wither' (Ak.Fa)	guŋguan / guŋŋuan

The phonological characteristics of the reduplicated forms of Type 1 CVC(V) stems are in some ways similar to those of CV stems.

a)   Like reduplicated forms of CV stems
    i)   the initial consonant of the stem is repeated
    ii)   the vowel of the prefix is a high vowel whether the vowel of the stem is high or not

iii) the vowel of the prefix has the same vowel harmony features as that of the reduplicated CV stem, that is the high vowel of the prefix agrees with the vowel of the stem in being advanced /unadvanced, rounded /unrounded as the case may be.

b) Where the second C is **w** or **r**, that is a non-nasal sonorant, the final syllable is not repeated in the prefix, exx. (10) to (14).

c) Where the second C is a nasal consonant,
i) the prefix has a CVN structure where N stands for a nasal consonant which is homorganic with (i.e. has the same place of articulation as) the following consonant, (exx. 15, 16, 18,19, 21-23)
ii) the prefix has a CV structure if the initial consonant of the verb is also nasal, as in examples 17 and 20.
iii) in the Akuapem and Asante dialects, if the initial consonant is a voiced plosive, this consonant is assimilated into a nasal, as in examples 19 and 23.

3. Reduplicated forms of Type 2 CVC(V) Stems

Type 2 CVC(V) stems reduplicate differently in Fante, Akuapem and Asante.

a) In **Fante**, where these stems have a CVC structure, the prefix of the reduplicated form may repeat the segmental sounds of the verb stem or drop the final consonant and geminate (or lengthen) the vowel of the first syllable. Both forms are used interchangeably, although the form with the long vowel in the prefix is likely to be used in less formal and less deliberate speech.

24 a.	sɔr	'get up'	sɔr*sɔr* / sɔɔ*sɔr*
25 a.	fir	'buy on credit'	fir*fir* / fii*fir*
26 a.	dãn	'turn over'	dãn*dãn* / dãã*dãn*
27 a.	mãn	'send food/money'	mãn*mãn* / mãã*mãn*

b) In **Akuapem** the reduplicated form is a repetition of the verb stem.

24 b.	sɔre	'get up'	sɔre*sɔre*
25 b.	firi	'buy on credit'	firi*firi*

| 26 b. | dan | 'turn over' | dan*nan* |
| 27 b. | mān | 'send food / money' | mãm*mān* |

c) In **Asánte** the prefix of the reduplicated form may either repeat the verb stem or drop the final syllable and geminate (or lengthen) the vowel of the first syllable as in Fante. Both are used interchangeably, although the form with the long vowel is likely to be used in less deliberate speech.

24 c.	sɔre	'get up'	sɔre*sɔre* / sɔɔ*sɔre*
25 c.	firi	'buy on credit'	firi*firi* / fii*firi*
26 c.	dānē /dāny	'turn over'	dānē*dānē* /dāā*dānē* /
			dāā*dāny*
27 c.	mānē /māny	'send food / money'	mānē*mānē* /
			māā*mānē* / māā*māny*

The reduplicated forms show that with Type 2 CVn(V) stems the following take place:

(1) The second consonant **n** is repeated even where the initial consonant is a nasal, ex. 27. (Compare Type 1 stems in 17 and 20.)
(2) In Fante a final nasal in the prefix is not necessarily homorganic with the following consonant.

Fa: man*man* *compare* Ak: mam*man* 'send food or money'

4. Reduplicated forms of other CVCV stems (incuding CCV)

a) The reduplicated forms of other CVCV stems are a repetition of the stem.

28.	kasa	'speak'	kasa*kasa*
29.	fitī	'pierce'	fitī*fitī*
30.	srɛ	'plead'	srɛ*srɛ*
31.	pra	'sweep'	pra*pra*
32.	furo	'crumble'	furo*furo*

b)   Where the disyllabic verb stem has an advanced vowel in the first syllable and the unadvanced open vowel **a** in the second syllable, the prefix has an advanced vowel in the second syllable. **e** is the advanced vowel that replaces **a** in the prefix, although in Akuapem and Asante, it is advanced **a** if the vowel is nasalised.

33.	bisa	'ask'	bise*bisa*
34.	kusā	'turn over'	kuse*kusā*
35.	gyīnā̄	'stop/stand'	gyīne*gyīnā̄* / gyīnā̄*gyīnā̄*

5.   Reduplicated forms of CVV stems

38.	sie	'hide'	sie*sie*
39.	bọa	'help'	bọa*bọa*
40.	mẹ̄ẹ̄	'eat enough'	mẹ̄ẹ̄*mẹ̄ẹ̄*
41.	daa	'deceive'	daa*daa*
42.	sɛẹ	'destroy'	sɛẹsɛẹ / sɛɛsɛẹ
43.	kaẹ	'remember'	kaẹ*kaẹ* / kaa*kaẹ*
44.	gyaẹ	'stop'	gyaẹ*gyaẹ* / gyee*gyaẹ*
45.	tsei	'listen' (Fa)	tsei*tsei* / tsee*tsei*
46.	kɔ̃ā	'bend'	kɔ̃ā*kɔ̃ā*
47.	tia	'step on'	tie*tia*

The phonological characteristics of th..se reduplicated forms are as follows:

a)   The prefix is a repetition of the stem where
   i)   where VV is a sequence of identical vowels, exx. 40, 41.
   ii) where VV is a sequence of a high vowel followed by a non-high vowel, exx. 38, 39, 46, 47.

b)   Where VV is a sequence of a non-high vowel followed by a high front vowel, examples 42 - 45, the prefix is either
   i)   a repetition of the stem or
   ii) the vowel sequence in the prefix is a repetition of the first vowel of the stem.

Both forms are used interchangeably, although the form with the long vowel, for example sɛɛsɛe̞ (42) is likely to be used in less formal and less deliberate speech than the form sɛe̞sɛe̞.

c) · In example 44, gyeegyae̞ has advanced vowels in the prefix of the reduplicated form because the following syllable is a palatal consonant followed by **a**.

d) Since the reduplicated form is basically a repetition of the stem, the vowels in the prefix are all advanced or unadvanced, nasalised or non-nasalised like the vowels of the stem.

e) Where the stem is 'mixed', that is, with a sequence of an advanced and the unadvanced vowel **a**, this vowel is replaced by **e** in the second syllable of the prefix, 44 and 47. Where the vowel is nasalised, the Akuapem and Asante forms sometimes have **a̰** in the prefix.

48. tĩã	'add'	tĩ ̄e*tĩã* / tĩ ̰a̰*tĩã*
49. hũã	'smell'	hũẽ*hũã* / hũa̰*hũã*

6. Reduplicated forms of other verb stems

50. kye̞rɛw	'write'	kyerɛ*kyerɛw* (Ak.Fa)
51. sunti	'stumble'	sunti*sunti*
52. patiri(w)	'slip'	pati*patiri(w)*
53. haram	'yawn'	hara*haram* / haraŋ*haram*
54. brantam	'be crooked'	branta*brantam* /
		brantam*mrantam*
55. mo̞nkye̞m	'twist'	monkye*monkyem*

The prefix in the above reduplicated forms basically repeats the stem, except that

i) stem-final **w** is not repeated, (compare CVw stems, exx. 10-12)

ii) in example 52 final **-ri(w**) is not repeated in the prefix (Compare Type1 CVrV stems, exx.13,14.)

iii) A stem-final nasal consonant may or may not be repeated in the prefix, if the initial consonant is not nasal. The reduplicated form in which the nasal is not repeated is the more frequently used one. Where the nasal is repeated in the prefix, it is homorganic with the following consonant, examples 53 and 54.

131

iv) Where the nasal is repeated in the prefix, a stem-initial voiced plosive is assimilated into a nasal in Akuapem and Asante, ex. 54.

v) A stem-final nasal is not repeated in the prefix if the initial consonant of the stem is also a nasal, ex. 55. (Compare Type 1 CVC(V) stems, exx. 17, 20.)

7. The Reduplication of reduplicated forms.

A verb stem may be reduplicated more than once. In theory, there is no limit to the number of times that a verb may be reduplicated, but in general, the largest reduplicated form in use is made up of three identifiable parts. If the simple stem is basically monosyllabic, that is, a CV or a Type 1 CVC(V) stem, each of the three parts will be more or less identical with the first reduplicated form. If the simple stem is any of the other stems, each of the three parts will be more or less identical with the simple stem.

	1st Red.	2nd. Red.	3rd Red.	
i) CV stem				
56.	bǫbɔ	bobɔ*bobɔ*	bobɔbobɔ*bobɔ*	'break'
57.	twi*twa*	twitwe*twitwa*	twitwetwitwe*twitwa*	'cut'

ii) Type 1 CVC(V) stems
58.	fi*fir(i)*	fifi*fifir(i)*	fifififi*fifir(i)*	'go out'
59.	tǫntɔn	tontɔ*tontɔn /*	tontɔtontɔn*tontɔn*	'sell'
		tontɔn*tontɔn*		
60.	kɛkaw	kekakekaw	kekakekakekaw	'bite'
61.	dun*dum /*	dundum*dundum /*	dundudundum*dundum /*	'extinguish'
	dun*num*	dunnu*dunnum*	dunnudunnu*dunnum*	
62.	mɛmǫnǫ	meme*memen /*	memememen*memen /*	'swallow'
		meme*memene*	memememe*memene*	

iii) Type 2 CVC(V) stems
	1st. Red.	2nd. Red.		
63.	sɔɔsɔr(e) /	sɔɔsɔɔsɔr(e) /		'get up'
	sɔrsɔr /	sɔrsɔrsɔr /		

	sɔresɔre	sɔresɔresɔre	
64.	dããdãn / (Fa)	dããdããdãn /	'turn over'
	dãndãn (Fa)	dãndãndãn	
	dããdãnē / (As)	dããdããdãnē /	
	dãnēdãnē (As)	dãnēdãnēdãnē	
	dannan (Ak)		

iv) Other CVCV stems

65.	bisebisa	bisebisebisa	'ask'
66.	frɛfrɛ	frɛfrɛfrɛ	'call'

v) Other stems

67.	kyerɛkyerɛw	kyerɛkyerɛkyerɛw	'write
68.	patipatiri(w)	patipatipatiri(w)	'slip'

These forms show the following features:

a) For CV and Type 1 CVC(V) stems, the whole of the first reduplicated form becomes the stem in subsequent reduplications, and the subsequent reduplicated forms reflect the features of such larger stems.

69.	twa	'cut'	twitwetwitwa
70.	tɔn	'sell'	tontɔtontɔn /tontɔntontɔn

In each example, the prefix in the first reduplicated form has a high vowel that agrees in two dimensions of vowel harmony (advanced/ unadvanced; rounded/unrounded) with the vowel of the stem. This is how CV and Type 1 CVC(V) stems reduplicate, (exx 1 - 23)

In the second reduplication, the prefix has the same features as prefixes in the reduplicated forms of CV(C)CV(C) stems.

71.	twitwetwitwa	is similar to	bisebisa	'ask'
72.	tontɔtontɔn/	is similar to	hyerɛhyerɛn /	'shine'
	tontɔntontɔn		hyerɛnhyerɛn	

Note : Where, as in Ak. As. dunnum*dunnum*, the stem final consonant is repeated in the prefix, this nasal is not homorganic with the following consonant, and if the stem begins with a voiced plosive, this plosive is not assimilated into a nasal consonant.

b) For other stems, the prefix is repeated in subsequent reduplications

72. bisebise*bisa*   'ask'
73. kyerɛkyerɛ*kyerɛw*   'write'

8. The tone of the Reduplicated Verb.

a) For CV and Type 1 CVC(V) stems,

  i) the prefix of the reduplicated form is said on Low tone, and the stem on High tone.

74. dà   :   dèdá   'sleep'
75. bɔ́   :   bòbɔ́   'break'
76. kà(ẁ) :   kèká(ẃ)   'bite'
77. tɔ̀n   :   tòntɔ́ń   'sell'
78. mèn(è, :   mèmén(é) 'swallow'

These reduplicated forms behave tonally like Group III disyllabic stems, (page 114 to 116).

  ii) The initial prefix of subsequent reduplicated forms has the same tone pattern as the first reduplicated forms above, but all syllables after this prefix are said on Low tone.

79. kèkákèkà(ẁ)   kèkákèkàkèkà(ẁ)   'bite'
80 tòntɔ́(ń)tòntɔ̀n   tòntɔ́tòntɔ̀tòntɔ̀n   'sell'

     as in ɔ̀kèkákèkà(ẁ)   'it (eg. a dog) keeps biting'
           ɔ̀tòntɔ́tòntɔ̀nèè   'he sold (eg. many things)'
           ɔ̀rèkèkákèkàkèkàẁ   'it is biting (in many places)'

134

b) For other stems, the initial prefix retains the tone pattern of the stem but syllables after this prefix are said on Low tone.

81.	pràpràprà	'sweep different places'
82.	fìrífìrì / fìifìr̀	'buy (many things) on credit'
83.	gyìnégyìnà	'stand (of many people)'
84.	bìsébìsèbìsà	'ask (many people / questions)'

as in	ɔ̀rèpràpràprà	'he is sweeping many places'
	òbìsébìsèbìsàè	'he asked many people / questions'

B Reduplicated Adjectives

The phonology of reduplicated adjectives is not as complex as that of reduplicated verbs.

There are basically two types of reduplication, one in which the stem is repeated once, and another in which the stem may be said to have been 'tripled'. This is true of CV and CVC stems.

85.	pá	'good'	pápá	pápáápá
86.	dɛ̀(ẁ)	'sweet'	dɛ̀dɛ́	dɛ̀déédɛ́ (Ak.)
			dɛ̀ɛ̀dɛ́	dɛ̀ɛ̀déédɛ́ (As.)
			dɛ̀ɛdɛ́ẃ	dɛ̀ɛ̀déédɛ́ẃ (Fa.)
87.	téń	'tall / long'	téńtéń	téńtééńtéń
88.	kɛ́tɛ̀(wá)	'small'	kétékété(wá)	kétékétékété(wá)

The phonological features of these reduplicated forms are as follows:

1) Where the stem is CV or CVC the reduplicated form may be
   (a) a repetition of the stem, or
   (b) if it is the 'tripled' form, the middle portion is a long vowel of the same quality as that of the stem. These long vowels may be analysed as a contracted form of a repeated stem. For example, papapapa is used as an alternative to papaapa.
2) If it is a CVCV stem, the reduplicated form is a repetition of the stem, as in example (88) above. (-wa is the diminutive suffix)

135

3) Tonally, if the stem is on High tone the reduplicated form tends to repeat this High tone on all the syllables, (exx. 85, 87, 88) but if it is on Low tone, the reduplicated form may have different tonal patterns in the different dialects, as in (86) above. Similar Low tone adjectives are fɛ̀ẁ 'beautiful', dèǹ 'hard'.

C   Reduplicated Nouns

Only plural forms of nouns may be reduplicated, and the reduplicated form is basically a repetition of the plural noun.

89. dúá	'tree'	ǹdùá (plural)	ǹdùéǹdúlá /
		ǹnùá	ǹnùéǹnúlá
90. àbòfŕá	'child'	m̀bòfŕá / (plural)	m̀bòfŕám̀bòfŕá /
		m̀mòfŕá	m̀mòfŕám̀mòfŕá

D   Functions of Reduplicated forms

Although it is possible to make up reduplicated forms for all verbs, adjectives and nouns on the basis of their phonological structure, not all verbs, adjectives and nouns have reduplicated forms in use in the language. For example the verb kɔ 'go' will reduplicate as kokɔ but this form is not in common use in the language. It occurs mainly in the language of children, on analogy with similar verbs like tɔ : totɔ 'buy'.

a) Verbs

The reduplicated verb inflects for person, tense and aspect like the simple unreduplicated verb stem, but it is used in different contexts to indicate the following:

1. A repetition of actions

bɔ	'to break'	bobɔ	'break up /hit repeatedly'
tu	'dig'	tutu	'keep on digging'

2. A plurality of subject

wu	'die'	wuwu	'die - of several persons'

136

3. A plurality of object

frɛ   'call'   frɛfrɛ   'call many people'

4. Sometimes a transitive verb becomes intransitive when reduplicated

di   'eat'   didi   'eat' - (without an object)

5. An intransitive verb may become transitive when reduplicated

da   'sleep'   deda   'put to sleep'

6. Sometimes the reduplicated verb has a slightly different meaning from the verb stem.

hwɛ   'look at'   hwehwɛ   'search'

hǫrǫ   'wash clothes'   hohoro   'wash up'

7. Some verbs are only used in in their reduplicated forms. They can be identified as reduplicated forms from their phonological structure even though there is no simple verb stem with related meaning.

daadaa   'deceive'   sesã   'change'

8. The reduplicated verb is more often used in nominalised forms than the simple verb root.

adidi(e)   'eating'   ɔkyerɛkyerɛfo   'teacher'

b) Adjectives

1. The reduplicated adjective indicates intensity, and the degree of intensity is related to the number of times the adjective is reduplicated.

papa   'good'   papaapa   'very good'

ketewa   'little'   keteketekete(wa)   'very, very tiny'

Where it is a plural adjective the whole of the plural form is reduplicated.

ahemfo akɛse	'important chiefs'
ahemfo akɛseakɛse	'very important chiefs'

2. Sometimes the simple adjective can only occur as a complement after the copula yɛ but the reduplicated form can occur in this position as well as after the noun as a modifier.

anoma no ho yɛ fɛ	'the bird is beautiful'
anoma fɛfɛ	'a beautiful bird'

3. The 'tripled' form of the adjective may also function as an adverb.

ɔayɛ no fɛfɛɛfɛ	'he has done it beautifully'

4. Like the verbs some adjectives are only used in their reduplicated forms.

tenten	'tall / long'

The stem ten does not occur by itself as an adjective, but it occurs in compounds like oguanten 'long -legged sheep'.

c)   Nouns

1. Reduplicated plural nouns merely emphasise the plurality of the noun.

bea(e)	'place'	mmea(e)	'places'
		mmeammea	'several places'

2. In a few cases the reduplicated noun functions as an adjective.

dua	'tree /wood'	nnuennua	'woody'

as in   bankye nnuennua   'rather woody cassava'

138

CHAPTER 6

SOUND CORRESPONDENCES BETWEEN AKUAPEM, ASANTE AND FANTE

I   INTRODUCTION

The following is a discussion of the major phonological processes (the changes and adjustments in sounds), which are characteristic of the Akan language. Some of these processes have been discussed in the earlier chapters. In this chapter attention will be drawn to those phonological processes which account for the differences in the distribution of consonants and vowels between the Akuapem, Fante and Asante dialects.

II   SOME PHONOLOGICAL PROCESSES IN AKAN

A   Vowel harmony

Vowel harmony is the restriction on the distribution of vowels which makes it necessary for Akan vowels to be grouped into two sets with only the vowels of one set co-occurring in any given word at a time. This has been discussed in detail in Chapter 1.

Basically, vowel harmony in Akan relates to how the two sets of vowels - 'advanced' vowels, i e ạ o u, and 'unadvanced' vowels, ọ ɛ a ɔ ọ, - do not normally occur together in the same word.

advanced vowels		unadvanced vowels	
obetu	'he will dig up'	ɔbɛtọw	'he will throw'
wạdidi	'he has eaten'	wagyẹ	'he has received'

The following are the differences between Akuapem, Asante and Fante that are due to the different ways in which the vowel harmony process operates in these dialects.

1.   In addition to the basic division between advanced and unadvanced vowels, Fante has another type of vowel harmony in which the vowels of some verbal prefixes and possessive pronouns agree with the vowels of

the stem in being back and rounded or front and unrounded as the case
may be.

a) Verbal prefixes

stem	Fante	cf.	Akuapem	Asante	
di	mirikedzi		merekodi	miikodi	'I'm going to eat'
tɛw	merekɛtsew		merekɔtew	meekɔte	'I'm going to pluck'
tu	murukotu		merekotu	miikotu	'I'm going to dig up'
tɔw	morokɔtow		merekɔtow	meekɔto	'I'm going to throw'

b)   1st and 3rd person possessive concord markers (pronouns)

Fante	cf.	Akuapem	Asante	
mi tsir		mi ti	mi ti	'my head'
ne nsa		ne nsa	ne nsa	'his /her hand'
nu nua		ni nua	ni nua	'his /her sibling'
mo kɔn		me kɔn	me kɔn	'my neck'

2. It was pointed out (pages 21-22) that one of the exceptions to the
vowel harmony rule is the fact that in the Akuapem dialect, the
Progressive prefix re always has an unadvanced vowel, whether or not
the stem has an advanced vowel. In such Progressive forms of the verb,
the subject-concord (pronoun) prefix that precedes the rɛ prefix also
has an unadvanced vowel. The examples in (a) above illustrate this point.
As can be seen from the examples, the Progressive prefix in Asante is
realised as a lengthening of the preceding vowel.

B Nasalisation

1. Nasalisation of vowels

As stated in Chapter 1, there are 5 nasalised vowels (the high and
low vowels), which occur independently nasalised after non-nasal
consonants.

In all dialects, the high vowels i ɛ ɔ u are nasalised when they
occur before nasal consonants, as shown in square brackets in the

following examples.

tim	[tĩm]	'be firmly fixed'
ben	[bẹ̃n]	'be cooked'
som	[sọ̃m]	'serve'
dum	[dũm]	'extinguish'

The non-high vowels are also nasalised before nasal consonants in Fante but not in Akuapem and Asante.

	Fante	Akuapem, Asante	
pam	pãm	pam	'sew'
fɛm	fɛ̃m	fɛm	'borrow'
kɔm	kɔ̃m	kɔm	'hunger'
bɛn	bɛ̃n	bɛŋ / bɛny	'be near'
tɔn	tɔ̃n	tɔŋ / tɔŋw	'sell'

2. Nasalisation of Consonants

a) Nasalisation of semivowels in Fante

As pointed out under nasalisation of vowels above, non-high vowels in Fante are nasalised when they occur before nasal consonants. It was also stated in Chapter 2 that semivowels in Akan do not occur before or after nasalised vowels. For these two reasons, Fante has nasal consonants in the following words where Akuapem and Asante have semivowels, in other words the nasalised vowel in the Fante forms assimilates the preceding semivowel into a nasal.

Fa:	nyãm	Ak.As:	yam		'grind'
	nyɛ̃n		yɛŋ / yɛny		'to rear'
	nwɔ̃n		wɛŋ / wɛny		'to watch'

b) Nasalisation of voiced oral consonants

In general, when a voiced oral (i.e. non-nasal) plosive or affricate is preceded by a homorganic nasal within the same word, the oral

141

consonant becomes nasal in Akuapem and Asante, but not in Fante.

Ak.As:		Fa:		
	mma		mba	'children'
	nnua		ndua	'trees'
	nnye		ngye	'not receive'
	nnwom		ndwom	'songs'
	ɔhemmaa		ɔhembaa	'woman chief'

The vowels that follow the assimilated consonant are not nasalised, however.

C   Homorganic nasal assimilation

In general whenever a nasal consonant occurs before another consonant within the same word in Akan, the nasal consonant has the same place of articulation as the following consonant. This can be illustrated by the following compounds

asɛm	'case'	kɛse	'big'	:	asɛŋkɛse	'big case'
kɔn	'neck'	pɔ(w)	'knot'	:	kɔmpɔ(w)	'goitre'

When a sequence of two consonants have the same place of articulation, they are said to be homorganic. In Akan nasals are usually homorganic with the following consonant when they occur in the same word. This is a regular phonological process in all the dialects of the language. Such words may be

i. Simple words :	ananse	'spider'
	buŋkam	'overshadow'
ii. Compounds :	asɛŋkɛse	'big case'
	kɔmpɔ(w)	'goitre'
iii. Plural forms of nouns :	mpanyimfo	'elders'
	ŋkoa	'fellows /slaves'
iv. Nouns not specified for number :	nsu	'water'
	mfɔte	'termites'

			ŋkran	'black ants'
v. Negative forms of verbs	:	ŋkɔ	'not go'
			nsu	'not cry'
			mfa	'not take'
vi. Optative forms of verbs	:	ɔŋkɔ	'let him go'
			memfa	'let me take it'

There are a few exceptions to this process.

a)   Before the nominal suffix -**fo**, nasals that occur after the vowel **a** are not homorganic with the following consonant.

Akan		:	Akanfo	'Akan people'
di kan	'lead'	:	adikanfo	'pioneers'
tan	'hate'	:	ɔtamʋ	'enemy'

b)   There are a few compounds in which homorganic nasal assimilation does not take place, as illustrated below.

nimdeε	'knowledge'	:	nim, adeε	'know', 'thing'
Fa: manman	'send food/money'	:	man	(reduplicated form)

D   Palatalisation

Palatalisation refers to the raising of the body of the tongue towards the hard palate when a sound is being made. For example **p** in **pɛ** 'like' is pronounced **pyɛ**, that is palatalised, in Fante, but **pɛ**, not palatalised, in Akuapem and Asante.

It was pointed out in Chapter 2 that in general, palatal consonants in Akan replace velar and glottal consonants before front vowels, and that the two groups of consonants complement each other in their distribution (page 47).

The replacement of a velar or a glottal sound by a palatal one before front vowels is a common phonological process in many languages. It is known as palatalisation, and it is the process whereby a more 'back' consonant such as **k** becomes progressively articulated on the hard palate under the influence of a following front (or palatal) vowel till it is

143

replaced by a palatal (or a 'front') consonant **ky**.

There are therefore two types of palatalisatiion in Akan - one in which a non-palatal consonant such as **p** has the front of the tongue raised during its articulation, as in Fante py**ɛ**, and another in which a non-palatal consonant such as **k**, is replaced with a palatal one, **ky**.

Palatalisation of consonants accounts for some of the differences between the three dialects under discussion, as illustrated below.

1.   Palatalisation of labial and alveolar consonants in Fante.

Labial and alveolar consonants in Fante are palatalised before front vowels. For alveolar stops palatalisation results in affrication, that is, the stops become affricates.

Fa: py**ɛ**	Ak.As: p**ɛ**	'like'
by**ẽn**	b**ẽn**	'be well cooked'
fy**ɛ̃m**	f**ɛm**	'borrow / lend'
ts**e̞w**	t**e̞w**	'pluck'
dzi	di	'eat'
ny**ĩm**	n**ĩm**	'know'

Note : a)   In Agona, a subdialect of Fante, **ts** is further palatalised into **ky**, as in the following examples:

Agona : ky**e̞w**	Fante :	ts**e̞w**	'pluck'
ky**ir**		tsir	'head'

b)   In the subdialect of Fante spoken in Elmina, **dz** is further palatalised into into **gy** in the word d**e̞** 'take'.

Elmina Fante	other Fante	
megye maa no	medze maa no	'I took it, gave it to him'
ɔgye aba	ɔdze aba	'he has brought it'

2.   Palatalisation of labialised consonants in Asante

In Asante, the labialised palatal consonants **dw**, **hw** correspond to

144

the labialised velar and glottal consonants spelt **gu** , **hu** in Akuapem and Fante, as illustrated below.

As:	Ak.Fa:	
dwa	gua	'split open / market'
dware	guar(e)	'have a bath'
hwā	huā	'beg for food'
hwām	huãm	'be fragrant'

As explained on page 21, **gu** and **hu** are articulated with advanced tongue root position, and are therefore further forward on the roof of the mouth than **g** and **h**. The fronting of these consonants as a result of the advanced tongue root position, accounts for the palatalisation in Asante.

E   Labialisation of consonants

Labialisation refers to the rounding of the lips when a sound is being made. For example, **kw** in ɔkwan 'road' is labialised, whereas **k** in kan 'read' is not.

In Akan, as in many languages, when a consonant is followed by a rounded vowel, that consonant takes on the lip-rounding of of the vowel and becomes labialised. For example, the **t** in tu 'dig' is labialised, while the **t** in tare 'adhere to' is not.

In Akan, this type of labialisation - brought about by a following vowel - is very noticeable in CVV stems where the first vowel is rounded and the second is not, as in noa 'cook', bue 'open'. In such stems the consonant may be

(1) Labialised, that is with protruding lips, as in pwei 'go out' (Fa)

or (2) Labial-palatalised, that is with the lips rounded while the body of the tongue is raised towards the palate, as in pɥie 'go out' (As)

One of the differences that can be observed between Akuapem, Asante and Fante relates to the type of labialisation that occurs with the initial consonant of CVV stems, as illustrated by tthe following examples. The spelling of the stems is given to the left

Stem		Fante	Akuapem	Asante
pue	'go out'	pwei	pue	pɥie
bue	'open'	bwei	bue	bɥie

145

nua	'siblibg'	nɥīã	nɥiã	nɥiã
dua	'tree'	dɥia	dɥia	dɥia
akuafo	'farmers'	ekwaafɔ	akɥiafɔ	akɥiafɔ
noa	'cook'	nɥē̃ã	nɥē̃ã	nō̃ã
toa	'join'	tɥęa	tɥęa	tɔa
aboa	'animal'	abɔa	abɔa /	abɔa
			abwęa	
moa	'gather'	mō̃ã	mō̃ã	mō̃ã
akoa	'fellow'	akɔa	akɔa	akɔa

As can be seen from the above examples, stem initial alveolar consonants are labial-palatalised in Akuapem in such stems. The velar consonant is labial-palatalised only if the first vowel is the advanced high back vowel. Labial consonants are normally not labialised in such stems, although the word for 'animal' has an alternative pronunciation where the initial bilabial plosive is labialised.

In Asante, the initial consonant is labial-palatalised only when the first vowel is the advanced high back vowel **u**.

In Fante, alveolar consonants in such stems are labial-palatalised. Labial and velar consonants are labialised where the first vowel of the stem is the advanced high back vowel **u**. Before the unadvanced high back vowel, labial and velar consonants are not labialised, as illustrated by the last three examples.

F   The rounding of vowels

1.   The rounding of vowels after labialised consonants

In the Asante and Fante dialects, there are some words in which back rounded vowels correspond to front unrounded vowels in Akuapem. The vowels in these words occur after labialised consonants, and the stems are all CVn(V),

Fa: nwin	Ak: nwin	As: nwunu	'shade'
nwęn	nwęn	nwɔnɔ	'weave'
ędwęn	dwęn	ɛdwɔnɔ	'grey hair'

146

twɔn	twɛn	twɛn	'wait'
nwɔn	wɛn	wɛn	'watch'

In Asante, the vowels that are rounded after labialised consonants are high vowels, while in Fante they are mid vowels. There are a few exceptions in Asante however, adwini, 'design' adwɛnɛ 'the mind'.

Akuapem is not affected by this phonological process whether it is a high or a mid vowel.

2. The rounding of vowels before final **w** in Fante

In some subdialects of Fante, there are words in which back rounded vowels correspond to front unrounded vowel in Akuapem, Asante and in some other Fante subdialects. The vowel in these words occur before word-final **w**. (Asante does not have word-final **w**)

Fa: tsɛw / tsɔw	Ak: tɛw	As: tɔ	'to tear'
kyɛw /kyɔw	kyɛw	ɛkyɛ	'hat'
ayɛw / ayɔw	ayɛ	ayɛ	'praise'

3. The rounding of vowels after labialised consonants and before final **w**

In Fante and in Akuapem, a high front vowel that occurs after a labialised consonant and before a final **w** may become rounded. Asante does not have word-final **w**, and the vowels in such stems are unrounded in Asante.

Ak.Fa: twiw / twuw	As: twi	'draw near'
dwiriw / dwuruw	dwi(ri)	'pull down'
dwiw / dwuw	dwie	'louse'

In Fante and Akuapem the pronunciation with the unrounded vowel **i** occurs in very careful speech.

G Vowel alternation in Asante

1. Verbs

In certain grammatical contexts - emphatic sentences and relative clauses - the vowels o ɛ o ɔ occurring in final position after r in Asante verbs correspond to i ọ u ọ in the same verbs when they occur in other grammatical contexts. Again this is unique to Asante.

<table>
<tr><td>ɔreforo dua</td><td>but</td><td>dua a ɔreforɔ no</td></tr>
<tr><td>'he is climbing a tree'</td><td></td><td>'the tree he is climbing'</td></tr>
<tr><td>ɔabeduru ha</td><td></td><td>ɛha na ɔabeduro</td></tr>
<tr><td>'he has arrived here'</td><td></td><td>'it is here that he has arrived'</td></tr>
<tr><td>ɔbɛkyekyere</td><td></td><td>ɔno na ɔbɛkyekyerɛ</td></tr>
<tr><td>'he will tie it up'</td><td></td><td>'it is he who will tie it up'</td></tr>
</table>

2. Before -i / -ẹ suffixes

It was observed in Chapter 4, page 94 that in Asante only, the mid vowels e and o are replaced by ɛ and ɔ respectively before the Past suffix and before the -i /-e nominal suffix.

wie	:	owiεẹ(ε)	'he finished'
		awiεẹε	'the end'
suro	:	osurɔẹ(ε)	'he was afraid'

H   Syllable reduction and syllable loss

1.   In stem words

As pointed out in Chapter 4, some CVCV stems have reduced CVC or CV forms., and this is one of the sources of the differences between the dialects, as illustrated by the following examples:

Fa:	Ak:	As:	
kyɛr	kyɛre /kyɛ	kyɛre /kyɛ	'delay'
sɔr	sɔre	sɔre	'get up'
hu	hu	hunu /hu	'see'
pen	pene	pene	'agree'
nyim	nim /ni	nimu / nim /ni	'know'
hom	home	home	'breathe'

dɔw	dɔw	dɔ	'weed'

The stems which undergo the process of syllable reduction and/or syllable loss are CVCV stems in which

i) the second consonant is a sonorant, i.e. **r n m w,**
ii) the final vowel is a high vowel, i.e. **I ɪ̣ ʊ̣ u,**
iii) the final syllable is said on Low tone. (See Chapter 4, page 113.)

2. Loss of nominal suffix

Another type of syllable loss can be observed in the presence of a vowel nominal suffix in Asante and its absence in Akuapem and Fante. The nominal suffix is a vowel which agrees with the vowel of the stem in being advanced/unadvanced and rounded/unrounded. Where the final vowel of the stem is a nasalised high vowel, the nominal suffix is a nasalised vowel of the same quality as that of the final vowel of the stem.

It is considered here that Akuapem and Fante have lost this suffix, in other words, the nominal suffix is not an innovation in Asante.

Fa:	adze	Ak:	ade	As:	adeɛ	'thing'
	siw		siw		esie	'anthill'
	ɔbo / boba		ɔbo		ɛboɔ	'stone'
	owu		owu		owuo	'death'
	ifĩ		efĩ		efĩĩ	'dirt'
	anọ̃		anọ̃		anọ̃ọ̃	'mouth'

I Final n in the three dialects

As explained in Chapter 4, the different pronunciations associated with CVn stems (reduced from CVnV) account for one of the differences between the three Akan dialects under consideration.

Fa:	bẽn	Ak:	bɛŋ	As:	bɛny	'be near'
	tõn		tɔŋ		tɔŋw	'sell'

149

J   Other dialect differences

1.   Asante nominal suffixes

a)   Suffixes in Asante nouns occur after stem-final short high vowel
and after **r**, where the Asante mid vowel suffixes correspond to final high
vowels in Akuapem.

As:	ɛwɔɔ	Ak:	ɛwo	Fa :	ewo	'honey'
	adeɛ		ade		adze	'thing'
	ɛberɛ		ɛbere		ber	'time'
	fifire		fifiri		fifir	'sweat'
	ɛborɔ		ɛbɔre		bɔr	'poison'
	aduro		aduru		edur	'medicine'

When inalienable nouns occur in possessive constructions, the
nominal suffix is deleted.

etire	'head'	but	Kofi ti	'Kofi's head'
nufoɔ	'breasts'	but	Ama nufo	'Ama's breasts'
akyire	'back'	but	m'akyi	'my back'

b)   Some Asante nouns have a mid vowel suffix when they occur in
emphatic sentences, and in relative and some other subordinate clauses
but have a final high vowel in other contexts, (cf. vowel alternation in
verbs above).

me na mekɔɔ Kumaseɛ	but	Kumase
'it is I who went to Kumasi'		
ɔbaa ɔfinsoɔ no	but	ɔfinso
'when he came to Ofinso'		
ɔbaa a ɔkɔɔ Oboguo no	but	Obogu
'the woman who went to Obogu'		

150

III SUMMARY OF DIALECT DIFFERENCES

The following is a summary of the dialect differences betweer Akuapem, Asante and Fante.

A Vowels

	Fante	Akuapem	Asante
1. Vowel harmony	mɪrɪkedzi	mɛrɛkodi	miikodi
(in verbal prefixes)	murukobu	mɛrɛkobu	miikobu
	mɔrɔkɔkɔ	mɛrɛkɔkɔ	mɛɛkɔkɔ
(in possessive	mi tsɪr	mi ti	mi ti
pronouns)	nɔ kɔn	nɛ kɔn	nɛ kɔn

2. Nasalisation of vowels

	pãm	pam	pam
	tɔ̃n	tɔŋ	tɔŋw

3. Rounding of vowels

(a)	twɔ̃n	twɛŋ	twɛny
	nwĩn	nwĩŋ	nwũnũ
(b)	kyɛw /kyɔw	kyɛw	kyɛ
	tsɛw / tsɔw	tɛw	te
(c)	twiw /twuw	twiw /twuw	twi
	dwiw /dwuw	dwiw /dwuw	dwie

B Consonants

1. Palatalisation of consonants

ts: t	tsew	tɛw	te	
dz: d	dzi	di	di	
ny: n	nyim	nim	nim	
gu: dw	guar	guare	dware	
hu: nw	huam	huam	hwam	

151

2. Nasalisation of consonants

mb: mm	mbu	mmu	mmu
nd: nn	nda	nna	nna
ŋg: ŋŋ	ŋgow	ŋŋow	ŋŋo
ngy: nny	ngye	nnye	nnye
ndw: nnw	ndwom	nnwom	nnwom
ny: y	nyãm	yam	yam
nw: w	nwɔ̃n	wɛn	wɛn

3. Final consonants

	pam	pam	pam
	hom	home	home
	sew	sew	se
	hor	horo	horo /ho
	kãn	kaŋ	kany
	dãn	daŋ	dane

4. Intervocalic d / r

	awar	aware	awadeɛ / awareɛ
		ɔkorow	korɔɔ / kodɔɔ

5. There are a few words in which Fante **d** corresponds to **s** in Akuapem and Asante. This is however *not* a regular sound correspondence between the dialects. It is limited to a few words only.

	do	so	so 'the top'
	dɛn	sɛn	sɛn 'how?'

C Affixes

1. Nominal prefixes	ẹdan / ɔdan	ɔdan	ɛdan
	ifie	ofi	efie
	egya	ạgya	ạgya

152

2. Nominal suffixes

adze	ado	adoɛ
iwu/owu	owu	owuo
ɪfɪ̄	efɪ̄	efɪ̄ɪ̄

3. Nominal suffixes in possessed nouns

m'ádàkàó	m'áldálká	m'àdákàá
mé hɔ̀hòó	mé lhɔ́lhó	mè hɔ́hòɔ́

4. Subject-concord verbal prefixes

ękɔ	wǫkɔ	wǫkɔ
ihu	wuhu	wuhu
ɔkɔ	ɛkɔ	ɛkɔ
wɔkɔ	mǫkɔ	mǫkɔ
wɔkɔ	wɔkɔ	yɛkɔ

5. Future Negative prefixes

ɔŋkɛfa /	ɔrǫmfa	ɔmfa
ɔrǫmfa /ɔmfa		

6. Past suffix

ɔfaǫ	ɔfaǫ		ɔfaǫ /ɔfaǫɛ
ohui	ohui		ohuì /ohùiɛ

CHAPTER 7

THE UNIFIED AKAN ORTHOGRAPHY

I   INTRODUCTION

The Akan language has for a long time had three different orthographies based on the three dialects Akuapem, Asante and Fante. In the early 1950's this state of affairs was considered unsatisfactory, for apart from the unnecessary cost of producing the same text in three different orthographies, it also limited the readership of books written in one or the other of the three orthographies.

An Akan Orthography Committee was set up in 1952 to work out a unified orthography for the language as a whole, so that a text written in Akan can be read without much difficulty by the Akuapem, the Asante and the Fante speaker. In 1978 the Committee arrived at decisions which will be the basis for the unified Akan orthography. The decisions were put together in a booklet 'Unified Akan Orthography' by the Bureau of Ghana Languages and the Language Centre of the University of Ghana.

What follows is a summary of the major decisions of the Committee. Much of the rationale behind these decisions has been explained in the section on phonological processes in the preceding chapter.

II   REPRESENTATION OF VOWEL HARMONY

1. In Verbal Affixes

Vowel harmony in verbal affixes has been fully represented in the Akuapem and Fante orthographies, but not in the Asante orthography.

Fante	Akuapem	Asante	
midzi	midi	medi	'I eat'
mefa	mefa	mefa	'I take'
obebisa	obebisa	ɔbebisa	'he will ask'
ɔbɔkɔ	ɔbɛkɔ	ɔbɛkɔ	'he will go'

This difference in representation is not always a reflection of a difference in pronunciation between the dialects. For example, the

Akuapem and Asante pronunciations for these forms are identical, as far as the vowel qualities are concerned.

In the unified Orthography vowel harmony will not be indicated in verbal prefixes, so that each verbal prefix will have the same spelling, as in the Asante examples above, irrespective of its pronunciation in any given word in any of the three dialects, as illustrated by the following examples.

Spelling	Pronunciation	
mefa	mɛfa (all dialects)	
medi	mɩdi (all dialects)	
mekɔ	mɛkɔ (Ak.As)	mɔkɔ (Fa)
mehu	mɩhu (Ak.As)	muhu (Fa)
ɔbɛfa	ɔbɛfa (all dialects)	
ɔbebisa	obebisa (all dialects)	
ɔbɛkɔ	ɔbɛkɔ (Ak.As.)	ɔbɔkɔ (Fa)
ɔbɛhu	obehu (Ak.As.)	obohu (Fa)
ɔabisa	wɛbisa (Ak.As.)	weebisa (Fa)

) Subject-concord prefixes

1st person singular	me	:	medi	'I eat'	mefa	'I take'
2nd pers. sing.	wo	:	wodi		wofa	
3rd pers. sing.	ɔ	:	ɔdi		ɔfa	
Impersonal	ɛ	:	ɛdi		ɛfa	
1st person plural	yɛ	:	yɛdi		yɛfa	
2nd person plural	mo	:	modi		mofa	
3rd person plural	wɔ	:	wɔdi		wɔfa	

) Tense and Aspect prefixes

Future	bɛ	:	ɔbɛdi	ɔbɛfa
Perfect	a	:	ɔadi	ɔafa
Progressive	re	:	ɔredi	ɔrefa

155

| Ingressive | 'going' | kɔ | : | ɔkɔdi | ɔkɔfa |
| | 'coming' | bɛ | : | ɔbɛdi | ɔbɛfa |

c) The verbal suffix - i /- ẹ

Vowel harmony will continue to be represented in the Past Tense suffix - i /-e

| ohui | 'he saw it' | ɔtae | 'he took it' |

3. Posessive-concord markers (possessive pronouns)

Vowel harmony will not be represented in the unified orthography.

me ti	'my head'	me dan	'my house'
wo nua	'your sibling'	wo kɔn	'your neck'
ne nua	'his sibling'	ne kɔn	'his neck'

3. Compounds

Vowel harmony in compounds will not be represented in the unified orthography, as illustrated by the following examples.

| abɔdin | 'title' | nsɛnhunu | 'useless talk' |

4. Fante **e**, Akupem and Asante **a**

In Akuapem and Asante **a** is the advanced vowel that corresponds to the unadvanced low vowel **a**. In Fante it is **e**, as in kạri / ker 'weigh'.
In the unified orthography only the Akuapem and Asante forms will be written.

| kari | 'weigh' | ɔahu | 'he has seen it' | agya | 'father' |
| baanu | 'two people' | Afua | 'a girl's name' | Kwaku | 'a boy's name' |

III REPRESENTATION OF TENSE / ASPECT AFFIXES

1. The Future prefix

In the first person singular of the Future verb the subject-concord prefix **me** and the Future prefix **bɛ** are pronounced **mɛ**. In the unified orthography the subject-concord prefix will be represented by **m** and the Future prefix will have the full form **bɛ**.

mbɛkɔ	pronounced	mɛkɔ	'I will go'
mbɛbisa	pronounced	mebisa	'I will ask'

2.   The Negative prefix

a)   The Negative form of verbs is indicated by a nasal prefix which is homorganic with (or has the same place of articulation as) the following consonant.
    Fante spelling normally represents this nasal prefix with two nasal consonant letters.

Fante		cf.	Ak. As.
ɔmmfa	'he doesn't take it'		ɔmfa (Ak.As)
ɔanntɔ	'he didn't buy it'		ɔantɔ (Ak.As)

    In the unified orthography the Negative prefix will be represented by one nasal consonant letter, as in the Akuapem and Asante examples above.

b)   Negative forms of the Optative (Imperative II) will be written with two nasal consonant letters - one representing the Negative, and the other for the Optative.

ɔmfa	'let him take it'	ɔmmfa	(Negative)
ɔntɔ	'let him buy it'	ɔnntɔ	(Negative)

c)   The Future Negative has different forms in the different dialects.

    Fa: ɔmfa / ɔremfa / ɔnkɛfa   Ak: ɔremfa   As: ɔmfa

    In the unified orthography the **re** and **kɔ** prefixes will not be represented, and the Futre Negative will be represented as follows:

ɔmfa	'he won't take it'	ɔndi	'he won't eat'

157

3. The Past Tense verb followed by an object or a complement

Where the Past Tense verb is followed by an object or a complement the final vowel or consonant letter of the verb will be doubled in the unified orthography. (See Chapter 4 Past Tense suffix, pages 94 -95.)

ɔtɔɔ bi	'he bought some'
ɔtɔnn bi	'he sold some'
ɔnomm bi	'he drank some'
ɔteww bi	'he plucked some'

IV REPRESENTATION OF PRONOUNS AND PRONOMINAL PREFIXES

1. In Chapter 4 (page 91) it was pointed out that Asante for example, has yɛn for both the 1st and 3rd person plural pronoun, and that Fante has hom not mo as the 2nd person plural pronoun. In the unfied Akan orthography only the following pronouns and pronominal prefixes will be represented.

1st person singular	me	:	me-
2nd person singular	wo	:	wo-
3rd person singular	ɔno	:	ɔ-
Impersonal	ɛno	:	ɛ-
1st person plural	yɛn	:	yɛ-
2nd person plural	mo	:	mo-
3rd person plural	wɔn	:	wɔ-

2. Asante 3rd person possessive concord marker (pronoun)

In the Asante dialect ɔ / o, not ne, is the 3rd person singular possessive concord marker for some kinship nouns (page 72).
In the unified orthography only ne will represent the 3rd person singular possessive concord marker, except in literary texts such as poetry and conversation pieces, where the Asante form may be needed for stylistic effects, in which case these forms will be written as follows:

158

o'nua   'his brother/sister'   ɔ'wɔfa   'his uncle'

where ɔ' represents an abbreviation of ɔno, the 3rd person singular pronoun.

V   ASANTE NOMINAL SUFFIXES

1.   After short vowels

Noun stems that end in a high vowel have a mid vowel nominal suffix in Asante.

adeɛ   'thing'   ɛwoɔ 'honey'   nsuo   'water'

In the unified orthography these nouns will be written without the suffix, that is ade, fi, nsu. However, the suffixed form will be written where it is needed for stylistic effects in literary texts such as poetry.

2.   After r

There are nouns in Asante in which a final mid vowel e ɛ o ɔ after r corresponds to a final high vowel in Akuapem. Such nouns end in r in Fante.

As: ɛberɛ	Fa: ber	Ak: bere	'time'
fifire	fifir	fifiri	'sweat'
ɛborɔ	bɔr	ɛbɔre	'poison'
aduro	edur	aduru	'medicine'

In the unified orthography, only the forms with the final high vowel, as in Akuapem, will be represented.

3.   In certain grammatical contexts

It was noted in Chapter 6, page 150, that in emphatic sentences and in relative clause constructions, Asante nouns end in a mid vowel suffix.

Kofi na ɔkɔɔ Kumaseɛ   'it is Kofi who went to Kumasi'

bere a ɔkɔɔ Kumaseɛ no   'when he went to Kumasi'

159

In the unified orthography these nouns will be written without the suffix in such constructions.

VI   VOWEL ALTERNATION IN VERBS

As was stated in Chapter 6 (page 148), that in certain grammatical contexts - in emphatic sentences and in relative clause constructions - CVrV verbs in Asante end in a mid vowel.

ɔreforo dua   dua a ɔreforɔ
   'he's climbing a tree'   'the tree he's climbing'
ɔabeduru ha   ɛha na ɔabeduro
   'he's arrived here'   'it is here that he has arrived'

In the unified orthography the forms with the mid vowels will not be written, that is these verbs will be written with the final high vowel in all contexts.

VII   ROUNDING OF VOWELS

1.   After labialised consonants

It was shown in Chapter 6 (pages 146 - 147) that in Fante and Asante back rounded vowels in some CVn(V) stems correspond to front unrounded vowels in Akuapem.   Such stems have initial labialised consonants.

        Fa: nwin   Ak: nwin   As: nwunu   'shade'

          twɔn   twɛn   twɛn   'wait'

In the unified orthography, rounding of vowels in these stems will not be represented, that is, only the forms with front vowels, as in Akuapem, will be written.

2.   Before final **w**

In some Fante subdialects back rounded vowels before final **w** correspond to front unrounded vowels in Akuapem and Asante, (page

147). In the unified orthography only the forms with front unrounded vowels will be represented.

sew	'sharpen'	kyɛw	'hat'	tew	'pluck'

3. After labialised consonants and before final **w**

In Akuapem and Fante high front vowels occurring after labialised consonants and before final **w** may be replaced in pronunciation with back rounded vowels, (page 147).

In the unified orthography only the forms with front vowels will be written.

twiw	'draw near'	dwiriw	'pull down'	dwiw	'louse'

VIII REPRESENTATION OF CERTAIN CONSONANTS

1. Fante alveolar consonants

It was pointed out under palatalisation that the alveolar consonants **t d n** in are replaced with **ts dz ny** respectively before front vowels in Fante.

In the unified orthography words in which these consonants occur will be written with **t d n**, and Fante speakers will read them with the appropriate consonant **ts dz** or **ny** as the case may be.

tew	'pluck'	di	'eat'	nim	'know'

2. Nasalisation of voiced plosives and affricates

In Akuapem and Asante voiced plosives and affricates are usually replaced with a nasal when they occur after nasal consonants within the same word, (pages 141-142)

In the unified orthography nasalisation of voiced plosives and affricates will not be represented, as in the examples below.

mba	'children'	ndi	'not eat'	ngye	'not receive'

Akuapem and Asante speakers will read these words with the

appropriate nasal consoriants.

3. Nasalisation of semivowels in Fante

As stated on page 141, semivowels are replaced in Fante with nasal consonants when they occur before nasalised vowels.
In the unified orthography, nasalisation of semivowels in this context will not be represented, as in the examples below.

yam,   'grind'   wɛn   'watch'   yɛn   'rear'

4. Representation of **nhw** as **nw**

The words for 'hair' and 'sand' are sometimes with **nhw** as in nhwi 'hair', at other times with **nw** as in nwi .
In the unified orthography, these words will be spelt with **nw**.

nwi   'hair'   **anwea**   'sand'

5. Final **w**

Words that end in final **w** in Akuapem and Fante will be written with this final consonant in the unified orthography. Asante speakers will read these words without the final consonant.

kaw   'bite'   tiw   'follow'   huw   'blow'

It is worth noting here that since semivowels in Akan occur with oral vowels only, the writing of these words with the final **w** eliminates the confusion that sometimes occurred in Asante spelling where words like **ka** 'bite' (with an oral vowel) and ka 'say' (with a nasalised vowel) were identical in spelling, since nasality of vowels in Akan is not indicated in the spelling.

6. Intervocalic **r / d**

In intervocalic position the Asante dialect often has **d** where the other dialects have **r**, as in

    As: **awadeɛ** / **awareɛ**   cf. Ak. Fa: **awar(e)**   'marriage'

162

In the unified orthography such words will be written with **r**.

ɔkorow   'wooden vessel'   **afiri**   'machine'   **ɔyare**   'illness'

IX   REPRESENTATION OF CVC(V) STEMS

1. CVrV stems

a)   In the discussion of CVrV stems in Chapter 4, pages103-104, the point was made that where the high front vowel **e** occurs betweenthe first consonant and **r,** this vowel is not pronounced, especially where the second vowel is a non-high vowel, except in very slow and deliberate speech.

      bra   'come'   **srɛ**   'plead'

In the unified orthography, such words (with a non-high vowel in the second syllable) will be written without the **e** vowel letter, as in the examples above. Other examples are

ɔbrɛ	'tiredness'	**fra**	'mix'
prɛte	'plate'	**srade**	'fat'
tra	'jump over'	**mprɛnsa**	'three'

However, words like

kyerɛ	'show'	**kyerɛw**	'write'
yera	'get lost'	**yeram**	'yawn'
werɛ	'heart / breast'	**yeraw**	'trouble'

which have traditionally been written with **e** between the two consonants will continue to be so written.

b)   All other CVrV stems will be written with a vowel letter between the first consonant letter and **r**. These are

i)   Stems in which **e** occurs before and after **r**.

      bere   'time / be red'   aberewa   'old woman'

| serew | 'laugh' | pere | 'struggle' |
| atere | 'spoon' | were | 'skin' |

ii)   Stems in which the first vowel is not e

fɛre	'be shy'	kyɛre	'delay'
ware	'be long/marry'	bɔre	'poison'
porɔw	'rot'	etiri	'head'
purow	'stumble'	aburow	'maize'
afuru	'stomach'	hwirew	'pierce'
atoro	'lies'	aborɔbɛ	'pineapple'

In the unified Akan orthography therefore, all Fante words which end in a final r like sɔr 'get up' edur 'medicine' will be written with a final vowel letter, and Fante speakers will read such words without the final vowel.

Exceptions to what has been stated above are

| kronkron | 'pure' | kronnyɛ | 'simplicitiy' |
| akron / nkron | 'nine' | | |

These words will continue to be written without a vowel letter between the first two consonants.

2.   CVnV stems

It was explained in Chapter 4 (page 108) that in the Akuapem dialect CVnV stems that basically have an oral vowel in the first syllable have a CVn structure and the final consonant is a velar nasal ; eg. ho° 'swell', and that those stems that basically have nasalised vowels have a CVnV structure, e.g. hono 'dissolve'. This distinction between oral and nasalised vowels in CVnV stems is not maintained in Fante and Asante. In Fante such stems end in a final n, and in Asante some of these words have two pronunciations - with and without the final vowel - as in men/mene 'swallow'.

In the unified orthography, the Akuapem spelling for these stems will be used.

a) Stems that end in a velar nasal ŋ in Akuapem will be written with a final **n**.

tɔn	'sell'	man	'turn'	hon	'swell'
pun	'expose to smoke'	ben	'be cooked'	nwen	'be hard'

b) All other CVnV stems will be written with a final vowel letter

hono	'dissolve'	hunu	'empty'	mene	'swallow'
nini	'male /python'	mana /	'send food /	gyina	'stand'
		mane	money'		

3. CVmV stems

It was pointed out in Chapter 4 (page 107) that where the stem ends in a final high vowel, the final vowel is not pronounced in Fante. In Akuapem and Asante the final vowel is not pronounced if it is a Type 1 stem, but where it is a Type 2 stem the final vowel may or may not be pronounced.

In the unified orthography the following spelling rules will apply.

a) All Type 1 stems (these are not prounnced with a final vowel in all dialects) will continue to be written without a final vowel letter.

hom	'press down'	dom	'bless'	pam	'sew'
fɛm	'borrow/lend'	bosom	'fetish'	kum	'kill'

b) All Type 2 stems that end in a final high front vowel will be written with the appropriate final vowel letter.

home	'breathe/rest'	dome	'curse'	gyimi	'be stupid'
kame	'withhold'	bosome	'moon'	tumi	'be able'

c) All Type 2 stems that end in a final high back vowel in some dialects, as in the following Asante examples.

| pamo | 'chase away' | **afrumu** | 'donkey' |
| **prɛmo** | 'cannon' | ɔframo | 'tree species' |

will be written without a final vowel letter.

| pam | 'chase away' | **afrum** | 'donkey' |
| ɔprɛm | 'cannon' | ɔfram | 'tree species' |

d)   All other CVmV stems will continue to be written with a final vowel letter.

| **soma** | 'send on errand' | **adwuma** | 'work' | **akoma** | 'heart' |

4.   CVwV stems : See page 162 (5) Final **w**

X   MISCELLANEOUS

1.   Names of the days of the week

It was pointed out in Chapter 4, page 80, that Asante has an affix vowel **a** that occurs between the two stems in the names of the days of the week, as in Kwasiada 'Sunday'

In the unified orthography only the forms without the affix, as in Akuapem and Fanʈe, will be written.

Kwasida	'Sunday'	Dwowda	'Monday'	Benada	'Tuesday'
Wukuda	'Wednesdav'	Yawda	'Thursday'	Fida	'Friday'
Memeneda	'Saturday'				

2.   In general, long vowels are represented by doubling the vowel letter. This practice is however not consistently followed where the long vowel occurs in the middle of the word, as in the spelling of **asase** 'earth'.

In the unified orthography long vowels in these words will be consistently written with two vowel letters.

| asaase | 'earth' | wɔfaase | 'niece/nephew' | ataade | 'dress' |

3. Word division

a) Linkers with sɛ / dɛ

The following expressions, which are sometimes written as one and at other times as two words, will be written as two words in the unified orthography.

efi /efiri sɛ / esiane sɛ / ɔnam dɛ   'because'

ɛsɛ sɛ / ɔwɔ dɛ   'there is need'

b) Compounds

The Akan Orthogrpaphy Committee's report shows, with examples, which expressions should be considered as copmpounds and therefore written as one word, and which expressions should not be so considered and therefore written as two or more words.

In general, where the resulting compound has undergone phonological change(s) (see Chapter 5), or where it is an idiomatic expression or an accepted term, it should be written as one word.

nkuranwi / nkuronwi	samanwi
'facial hair'	'hair on a child at birth'
Benkumhene	sukwan
'a sub-chief'	'path leading to a water- collecting point'
Mamfehene	adansekurum
'chief of Mamfe'	'false witness'
abakɔn	burodua
'wrist'	'corn cob'
ayeforokunu	ɔsɔfopanyin
'bridegroom'	'Bishop / senior pastor'

For a detailed discussion of different types of compounds and how they should be written, see the report 'The Unified Akan Orthography'.

SELECT BIBLIOGRAPHY ON AKAN PHONOLOGY

Abakah, E.N. (1978) 'Dialect differences between Iguae Fantse and Bɔrbɔr (Nkusukum) Fantse'. Unpublished Long Essay, Department of Linguistics, University of Ghana, Legon.

Adjaye. S.A. (1984) 'Fante : the orthography versus speech' *Papers in Ghanaian Linguistics*, No.4, Institute of African Studies, Legon.

Akrofi, C.A. (1937, 2nd ed.1943) *Twi Kasa MMara* (Twi Grammar). Longman, London.

Akrofi, C.A. and Rapp, E.L. (1939) *Twi Nsɛm Nkorɛnkorɛ Kyerɛwbea* (Twi spelling book) Government Printing Office, Accra.

Andoh-Kumi, K. (1971) 'A pilot dialect geography of Agona'. Unpublished Long Essay, Department of Linguistics, Legon.

Andoh-Kumi, K. (1979) *Akan Kasa Nnyegyeeɛ Ho Adesua bi* (A Phonology of Akan) Mimeograph, University of Cape Coast.

Balmer, W.T. and Grant, F.C.F. (1929) *A Grammar of the Fante-Akan Language* Atlantis Press, London.

Bartels, F.L. and Annobil, J.A. (1946) *Mfantse Nkasafua Dwumadzi (A Fante Grammar of Function stages 1,2 &3)* Methodist Book Depot, Cape Coast.

Berry, J. (1957) 'Vowel Harmony in Twi', *Bulletin of the School of Oriental and African Studies, 19.*

Berry, J. (1960) *English, Twi, Asante, Fante Dictionary.* McMillan, London.

Boadi, L.A. (1963) 'Palatality as a factor in Twi Vowel Harmony'. *Journal of African Languages, 2*, Part 2.

Boadi, L.A. (1966) The syntax of the Twi verb. Ph.D. thesis, University of London.

Boadi, L.A. (1974) 'Nzema-Ahanta Medial /k/ and its reflexes in other Volta-Comoe languages' *Archivum Linguisticum.*

Boakye, P. (1981) *Syntaxe de l'achanti: du phonéme à la phrase segmenteé.* Publications Universitaires Europeénnes, Serie 21, Linguistique, Vol.19, Berne. Peter Lang.

Cahill, M. (1985) An autosegmental analysis of Akan nasality and tone. Unpublished project paper, University of Texas at Arlington.

Christaller, J.G. (1875) *A Grammar of the Asante and Fante Language called Tshi (Chwee, Twi).* Basel., Basel Evangelical Society.

168

Christaller, J.G. (1881, 2nd ed. 1933) *A Dictionary of the Asante and Fante Language called Tshi (Twi)*. Basel, Basel Evangelical Society.

Clements, G.N. (1981) 'Akan Vowel Harmony : a non-linear analysis'. *Harvard Studies in Phonology 2*, Bloomington, Indiana University Club.

Clements, G.N. (1984) 'Vowel Harmony in Akan : a considerstion of Stewart's word structure conditions' *Studies in African Linguistics*, 15. 3.

Dolphyne, F.A. (1965)   The Phonetics and Phonology of the verbal piece in the Asante dialect of Twi. Ph.D. thesis, University of London.

Dolphyne, F.A. (1967) 'A phonological analysis of Twi vowels' *Journal of West African Languages IV.*

Dolphyne, F.A. (1971) 'A classification of Akan verb stems' *Actes du 8e Congres de la Societe Linguistique Occindentale*, Abidjan.

Dolphyne, F.A. (1976a) 'Delafosse's Abron wordlist in the light of a Brong dialect survey' *Communication from the Basel Africa Bibliography* Vol. 14.

Dolphyne, F.A. (1976b) 'Dialect differences and historical processes in Akan' *Legon Journal of the Humanities*, Vol.III.

Dolphyne, F.A. (1979) 'The Brong (Bono) dialect of Akan' *Brong Kyempem*, ed. K. Arhin, Afram Publications, Accra.

Dolphyne, F.A. (1982) 'Akan language patterns and development' *Tarikh : Akan History and Culture*, Vol.7, No.2. Longman.

Dolphyne, F.A. (1984) 'Syllable reduction and syllable loss in tone languages' *Papers in Ghanaian Linguistics*, No.4, I.A.S. University of Ghana, Legon.

Dolphyne, F.A. (1986) 'Tone and grammar in Akan: the tone of possessive constructions in the Asante Dialect' *The Phonological Represenation of Suprasegmentals*, Holland Foris Publications, Dordrecht. K. Bogers, H. van der Hulst & M. Mous eds

Dolphyne, F.A. (1987)   'The phonetics and phonology of downstepped high tones' Paper read at the 18th Conference on African Linguistics, Montreal.

Forson, B. (ed) (1978) The Unified Akan Orthography.   Mimeograph, Legon

Fromkin, V.A. (1977) 'The Phonology of Akan revisited' in F.A. Kotey & Haig der Housikian , eds. *Language and Linguistic Problems in Africa*. Proceedings of the 7th Congress on African Linguistics, Columbia. S.C. Hornbeam Press.

Lindau, M. (1979) 'The Feature Expanded', *Journal of Phonetics*, 7.

Mensah, E.N.A. (1973) Les Consonnes Fanti. Etude Radiocinemato-
graphique. Implications phonologiques. These de Doctorat
3eme cycle. Biblioteque Nationale, Strassbourg.

Mensah, E.N.A. (1977) 'Problems of palatalisation in Akan' *Papers in
Ghanaian Linguistics* 2, I.A.S. Legon, Ghana.

Mensah, E.N.A. (1982) The Feature Lingual and the Akan consonant
system' *JWAL*, 12. 1.

Menscer, G. (1981) 'The tone structure of Asante disyllabic verb stems'.
Unpublished Long Essay, Department of Linguistics, Legon,
Ghana.

Nketia, J.H. (no date) *The Writing of Twi : Asante Speling.* Accra.

Nyaggah, L. (1976) 'Associative tone and syllable structure in Asante Twi'
Studies in African Linguistics. Supplement 6.

Redden, J.E., Owusu, N. et al. (1963) *Twi Basic Course* Foreign Service
Institute, Washington D.C.

Schachter, P. (1961) 'Phonetic similarity in tonemic analysis, with notes
on the tone system of Akuapem Twi' *Language* 31, No. 2.

Schachter, P. and Fromkin, V. (1968) A Phonology of Akan : Akuapem,
Asante and Fante *Working Papers in Phonetics* No. 19, UCLA.

Schachter, P. (1969) 'Natural assimilation rules in Akan' *IJAL* Vol. xxxv.

Stewart, J.M. (1963a) An analysis of the structure of the Fante verb, with
special reference to tone and glottalisation. Ph.D. thesis,
University of London.

Stewart, J.M. (1963b) 'Twi tenses in the Negative' *Actes du 2eme
Colloque internationale de linguistique negro-Africaines.* Dakar
University.

Stewart, J.M.(1965) *The typology of the Twi tone system* (with comments
by P. Schachter and W.E. Welmers) I.A.S., Legon.

Stewar, J.M. (1966a) 'Akan history, some linguistic evidence' *Ghana
Notes and Queries* No.9.

Stewart. J.M. (1966b) 'Asante Twi in the Polyglotta Africana' *Sierra Leone
Language Review* 5.

Stewart, J.M. (1966c) 'A deep phonology of the Akan monosyllabic stem'
(Paper presented at the 7th West African Languages Congress,
Yoaunde) I.A.S. Library, Legon.

Stewart,J.M. (1966d) 'Some suggestions for a Unified Akan Orthography'
Unpublished paper. I.A.S. Library, Legon.

Stewart, J.M. (1967) 'Tongue root position in Akan vowel Harmony'
Phonetica, 16.

Stewart, J.M. (1970) 'A theory of the origin of Akan vowel harmony'
*Proceedings of the 6th International Congress of Phonetic
Sciences* Czechoslovak Academy of Sciences, Prague.

Stewart, J.M. (1972) 'The Languages' *Akwapim Twi* ed. D. Brokensha. Ghana Publishing Corporation, Accra.

Stewart, J.M. (1976) 'The final light syllables of Akan (Twi-Fante) and their significance for Volta-Comoe reconstruction' *Communications from Basel Africa Bibliography*. Vol.14.

Stewart, J.M. (1983a) 'Akan vowel harmony: the word structure conditions and the floating vowels' *Studies in African Linguistics*, 14.2.

Stewart, J.M. (1983b) 'The Asante Twi tone shift' in I. Dihoff ed. *Current approaches to African Linguistics* Vol.1.R. Dordrecht. Foris.

Tufuor, Y. (1982) 'Le downstep "automatique" a la lumiere du Twi': l'instrumentation a la service de la linguistique' *Cahiers Inoirens de Recherche Linguistique* 2.

Ward, I.C. (1939) *The Pronunciation of Twi* Cambridge, Heffer.

Welmers, W.E. (1946) *A Descriptive Grammar of Fanti* supplement to *Language* 22, 3.

Welmers, W.E. and Harris, Z.S. (1942) 'The phonemes of Fante' *Journal of American Oriental Society*', 62.

Yankah, K. (1973) 'The sociolinguistic factor in the use of Agona /ts/' Unpublished Long Essay, Linguistics Department, Legon.

Language Centre & Bureau of Ghana Languages (1978) The Unified Akan Orthography. Mimeograph.

Methodist Book Depot, Cape Coast (1942) *Mfantse Nkasafua Nkyerɛwee nye ho Mbra* (Fante wordlist with principles and rules of spelling)

Methodist Book Depot, Cape Coast (1955) *Mfantse Nkasafua Nkyerɛkyerɛase* (Fante-English Dictionary)

Methodist Book Depot, Cape Coast. (1950) *Twi Nsɛm Dwumadie* (A Twi Grammar of function)

THE VERBAL PARADIGM

The following shows the 10 Tense/Aspect (Ingressive and Non--Ingressive) forms of the verb with their tone patterns for Akuapem, Asante and Fante.

As indicated in Chapter 4, (pages 111-115) the Akan verb stem has four basic tone patterns associated with it. The four basic tone patterns are illustrated below as follows:

A. Monosyllabic stem .... da   'sleep'

B. Disyllabic : Tone Group I stem .... tɔn   'sell'

C. Disyllabic : Tone Group II stem .... gyina   'stop / stand'

D. Disyllabic : Tone Group III stem ...... bisa   'ask'

The spelling of the verbal forms below are in accordance with decisions on the unified Akan orthography. Tone is not marked in Akan orthography, but the tone patterns are given for the verbs in this Appendix as a guide to the pronunciation of the verbal forms.

In general, there are two tone patterns associated with each Tense/Aspect form, one for the 1st and 3rd persons of the verb, (both singular and plural) and another for the 2nd person singular and plural forms. The Habitual forms for **da** below give all the persons of the verb. Subsequent verbal forms in this Appendix only give the singular forms of the verb to illustrate the two tone patterns.

I   NON-INGRESSIVE FORMS

A   Monosyllabic stem : da 'sleep'

da is a Low tone stem, but as pointed out in Chapter 4 (pages 111-112) the difference between High tone and Low tone monosyllabic stems is consistently carried by only the Progressive Affirmative and Past Negative forms of the verb in Asante. This means that the tone patterns given for **da** are for the most part the same for all CV stems. Where the tone pattern for a High tone verb is different from what is given for **da**, the pattern for **ba**, a High tone verb, is also given.

1. Habitual

Affirmative		Negative	
médà (Ak.Fa)	mèdá (As)	mènda̋ (Ak.Fa)	mèndà (As) *
wódà	wódá	wóndá	wóndà
ɔ́dà	ɔdá	ɔ̀ndá	ɔ̀ndà
ɛ́dà	ɛdá	ɛ̀ndá	ɛ̀ndà
yɛ́dà	yɛ̀dá	yɛ̀ndá	yɛ̀ndà
módà	módá	móndá	móndà
wɔ́dà	wɔ̀dá	wɔ̀ndá	wɔ̀ndà

* In Asante the tone pattern for a High tone verb ba is the
same as the Ak. & Fa. Negative forms :   mèmbá
                                         wómbá
                                         ɔ̀mbá etc.

2. Stative (not all verbs occur in this paradigm)

mèdà	mèndá
wódà /wòdà (Fa)	wóndá /wòndá (Fa)
ɔdà	ɔ̀ndá

3. Past

Ak.Fa.	As.	Ak.Fa.	As.
(a) mèdáè	mèdàè	màndá	màndà
wóldáè /	wódàè	wóándá /	wóándà
wòdáè (Fa)		wòàndá (Fa)	
ɔdáè	ɔdàè	ɔ̀àndá	ɔ̀àndà

*Note: cf. below Asante High tone verb ba (same as for Ak. & Fa.)

(b) mèdáà	mèdàà	ba :	màmbá
wóldáà/	wódàà		wóàmbá
wòdáà (Fa)			
ɔdáà	ɔdàà		ɔ̀àmbá

173

4. Perfect

Ak.Fa.	As.		Ak.As.	Fa.
m̀aádà	m̀adá	(a)	mèndaê	méndaê
wóádà	wóáldà		wónldaê	wóndaê
ɔ́ádà	ɔ̀adá		ɔ̀ndaê	ɔ́ndaê
Fa.* m̀aádá		(b)	mèndaâ	méndaâ
wóádá			wónldaâ	wóndaâ
ɔ́ádá			ɔ̀ndaâ	ɔ́ndaâ

*(Fante has two tone patterns in the Affirmative)

5. Progressive

Fa.	Ak.	As.*	Fa.Ak.	As.*
m̀erédá	m̀erédà	m̀eredà	méréndá	méréndà
wòrédá	wólrédà	wóredà	wóréndá	wóréndà
ɔ̀redá	ɔ̀rédà	ɔ̀redà	ɔ́réndá	ɔ́réndà

* compare Asante High tone verb **ba**

m̀erèbá	mérémbá
wórèbá	wórémbá
ɔ̀rèbá	ɔ́rémbá

6. Future I (Indefinite Future)

	Ak.Fa.	As.	(As)*
mbɛdá	méndá	méndà	mémbá
wóbɛdá / wòbɛdá (Fa)	wóndá	wóndà	wómbá
ɔ̀bɛdá	ɔ́ndá	ɔ̀ndà	ɔ́mbá

*Asante tone pattern for High tone verb **ba**

7. Future II (Immediate Future)

		Negative
mèrèbédá (Fa)	mèrèbèdá (Ak.As)	same as for Future I
wòrèbédá	wórèbèdá	
ɔrèbédá	ɔrèbèdá	

8. Consecutive *

	Ak.Fa.	Fa.	As.		Ak. Fa.	As.
				Negative : see also **Note** below.		
(na)	màádà	màádá	màdá	(na)	màndá	màndà
	wóádà	wóádá	wóáldá		wóàndá /	wóàndà
	ɔádà	ɔádá	ɔàdá		wòàndá (Fa)	
					ɔàndá	ɔàndà

(tone pattern for Negative Asante High tone verb **ba**, same as for Negative Akuapem and Fante **da**)

* The Consecutive verb does not occur by itself, but occurs as a non-initial verb in a serial verb construction in which the first verb is in the Progressive or in the Future tense.

a) Progressive : ɔretɔ nsa <u>akɔ</u> akuraa <u>akɔtɔn</u>
'he's buying drinks to take to the village to sell '

b) Future I : ɔbɛtɔ nsa <u>akɔ</u> akuraa <u>akɔtɔn</u>
'he will buy drinks to take to the village to sell '

c) Future II: ɔrebɛtɔ nsa <u>akɔ</u> akuraa <u>akɔtɔn</u>
'he's about to buy drinks to take to the village to sell '

Note: The Negative of these sentences are as follows :

i) ɔrentɔ (Prog.) / ɔntɔ (Fut.) nsa <u>nkɔ</u> akuraa <u>nkɔtɔn</u>
or
ii) ɔrentɔ (Prog.) / ɔntɔ (Fut.) nsa na <u>ɔakɔ</u> akuraa <u>akɔtɔn</u>
'he's not buying / he will not buy drinks to take to the village to sell '

In sentence (i) the negative of the Consecutive verb is the same as for the Future. In sentence (ii) only the first verb is negated; the Consecutive verb remains in the Affirmative. There is no meaning difference between the two sentences.

This means that there is no Negative form that directly corresponds to the Consecutive Affirmative in these sentences.

The following Negative forms,

na manda

na woanda

na ɔanda   etc.

that are given above and in textbooks such as the Twi Spelling Book (Twi Nsɛm Nkorɛnkorɛ Kyerɛwbea), as the Consecutive Negative forms, occur in sentences such as the ones below:

ɔbɛnom kɔfe na ɔanda
'he will drink coffee so that he will not sleep'

dua no yiye na ɛantutu angu
'plant them well so that they do not get uprooted'

These sentences are the negative of the following :

ɔnnom kɔfe na ɔada
'he will not drink coffee so that he will sleep'

ndua no yiye na ɛatutu agu
'do not plant them well so that they get uprooted'

This means that the Negative form of the Consecutive verb, as given in Akan verbal paradigms in this Appendix and elsewhere, negates the Affirmative Consecutive verb only when it occurs in a subordinate purpose clause, as in the above examples. However, in the general environment of a serial verb construction, in which the Consecutive verb normally occurs, the affirmative Consecutive does not have a corresponding negative form.

9.   **Imperative I** (Simple Imperative)

dá   ńdá / m̀má ńdá (Fa)

10. Imperative II (Optative)

(mà)	méńdá	(m̀ma)	mèńǹdá (Ak.Fa)	mèńǹdà (As)*
	ɔ́ńdá		ɔ̀ńǹdá	ɔ̀ńǹdà
	yɛ́ńdá		yɛ̀ńǹdá	yɛ̀ńǹdà
	móńdá		móńǹdá	móńǹdà
	wɔ́ńdá		wɔ̀ńǹdá	wɔ̀ńǹdà

> * Asante tone pattern for the High tone verb **ba** is the same as for the Ak. & Fa. Negative for **da** above.

Note: Traditionally the 2nd person plural form **monda** is included under Imperative I, but as can be seen from the above examples, it has the nasal prefix and the tone pattern of Imperative II.

B Disyllabic Tone Group I : tɔn 'sell'

As indicated on page 113, there are two types of Group I stems - Low-Low and High-Low. **tɔn** is a Low-Low stem. The tone pattern for **nom**, 'drink' a High-Low stem, will be given where it is different from that for **tɔn**

1. Habitual

métɔ̀n (Ak.Fa)	mètɔ́ń (As)	mèǹtɔ́ń (Ak.Fa)	mèǹtɔ̀n (As)*
wótɔ̀n	wótɔ́ń	wòǹtɔ́ń /	wòǹtɔ̀n
ɔ́tɔ̀n	ɔ̀tɔ́ń	wòǹtɔ́ń (Fa)	
		ɔ̀ǹtɔ́ń	ɔ̀ǹtɔ̀n

> * The tone pattern for a High-Low stem **nom** is the same as for the Ak. & Fa. Negative forms.

2. Stative (not all verbs occur in this paradigm)

mètɔ̀n		mèǹtɔ́ń
wótɔ̀n / wòtɔ̀n (Fa)		wòǹtɔ́ń
ɔ̀tɔ̀n		ɔ̀ǹtɔ́ń

177

3. Past

(a) mètɔ́nèè (Ak.Fa)   mètɔnèè (As)   màntɔ́ń (Ak.Fa)   màntɔ̀ǹ (As)*

    wóltɔ́nèè /   wótɔnèè   wóàntɔ́ń /   wóàntɔ̀ǹ

    wòtɔ́nèè (Fa)   wòàntɔ́ń (Fa)

    ɔ̀tɔ́nèè   ɔ̀tɔnèè   ɔ̀àntɔ́ń   ɔ̀àntɔ̀ǹ

* Asante Negative for High-Low stem nom same as above for Ak. & Fa.

(b) mètɔ́ńń   mètɔ̀ǹǹ

    wótɔ́ńń /   wótɔ̀ǹǹ

    wòtɔ́ńń (Fa)

    ɔ̀tɔ́ńń   ɔ̀tɔ̀ǹǹ

4. Perfect

Ak.Fa	As		Ak.As	Fa
màátɔ̀ǹ	màtɔ́ń	(a)	mèntɔ́néè	méntɔ́nèè
wóátɔ̀ǹ	wóáltɔ́ń		wóntɔ́néè	wóntɔ́nèè
ɔ̀átɔ̀ǹ	ɔ̀àtɔ́ń		ɔ̀ntɔ́néè	ɔ́ntɔ́nèè
		(b)	mèntɔ̀ǹǹ	méntɔ̀ǹǹ
			wóntɔ̀ǹǹ	wóntɔ̀ǹǹ
			ɔ̀ntɔ̀ǹǹ	ɔ́ntɔ̀ǹǹ

5. Progressive

Ak.Fa.	As.*		
mèrétɔ̀ǹ	mèrètɔ̀ǹ	mérèntɔ́ń	mèrèntɔ́ń (Fa)
wólrétɔ̀ǹ /	wórètɔ̀ǹ	wórèntɔ́ń	wórèntɔ́ń
wòrètɔ̀ǹ (Fa)		ɔ́rèntɔ́ń	ɔ̀rèntɔ́ń
ɔ̀rétɔ̀ǹ	ɔ̀rètɔ̀ǹ		

* cf. Asante High-Low Stem nom   1(Fante has both tone patterns in

      mèrènóm   the Negative)

      wórènóm

      ɔ̀rènóm

6. Future I

mbétɔ́ń	méǹtɔ́ń (Ak.Fa)	méǹtɔ̀ǹ (As) *
wóbétɔ́ń / wòbétɔ́ń (Fa)	wóǹtɔ́ń	wóǹtɔ̀ǹ
ɔ̀bétɔ́ń	ɔ́ǹtɔ́ń	ɔ́ǹtɔ̀ǹ

* Asante tone pattern for the Negative of a High-Low verb nom is the same as the Ak. & Fa. forms

7. Future II

Fa.	Ak.As.	Negative
mèrèbétɔ́ń	mèrèbɛ̀tɔ́ń	(same as for Future I)
wòrèbétɔ́ń	wórèbɛ̀tɔ́ń	
ɔ̀rèbétɔ́ń	ɔ̀rèbɛ̀tɔ́ń	

8. Consecutive

	Ak.Fa.	As.		Ak. Fa.	ᴧs.*
(na)	màátɔ̀ǹ	màtɔ́ń	(na)	màǹtɔ́ń	màǹtɔ̀ǹ
	wóátɔ̀ǹ /	wóáltɔ́ń		wóáǹtɔ́ń	wóáǹtɔ̀ǹ
	wòàtɔ̀ǹ (Fa)			wòàǹtɔ́ń (Fa)	
	ɔ́átɔ̀ǹ	ɔ̀àtɔ́ń		ɔ̀àǹtɔ́ń	ɔ̀àǹtɔ̀ǹ

* Asante Negative for High-Low stem nom same as Ak. Fa. forms above. See also **Note** on the Negative, pages 175-176.

9. Imperative I (Simple)

tɔ́ń	ǹtɔ́ń / m̀má ǹtɔ́ń (Fa)

10. Imperative II (Optative)

(mà)	méǹtɔ́ń	(m̀má)	mèǹǹtɔ́ń (Ak.Fa) méǹǹtɔ̀ǹ (As)*
	ɔ́ǹtɔ́ń		ɔ̀ǹǹtɔ́ń ɔ̀ǹǹtɔ̀ǹ

* Negative of High-Low stem nom same as for Ak. & Fa

C Disyllabic Tone Group II : gyina 'stop / stand'

1. Habitual

mègyìná   mèǹgyìná
wógyìná / wògyìná (Fa)   wóǹgyìná / wòǹgyìná (Fa)
ɔ̀gyìná   ɔ̀ǹgyìná

2. Stative

mègyìnà   mèǹgyíná (Ak.As)   mèǹgyínà (Fa)
wógyìnà / wògyìnà (Fa)   wóǹ!gyíná   wòǹgyínà
ɔ̀gyìnà   ɔ̀ǹgyíná   ɔ̀ǹgyínà

3. Past

(a) mègyìnáè (Ak.As)   mègyínàè (Fa)   màǹgyìná
    wógyìnáè   wògyínàè   wóáǹgyìná /
                                            wòàǹgyìná (Fa)
    ɔ̀gyìnáè   ɔ̀gyínàè   ɔ̀àǹgyìná
(b) mègyìnáà   mègyínàà
    wógyìnáà   wògyínàà
    ɔ̀gyìnáà   ɔ̀gyínàà

4. Perfect

Ak.As.	Fa.		Ak. As.	Fa.
màgyíná	màagyíná	(a) mèǹgyínáè	méńgyínáè
wóá!gyíná	wóágyíná	wóǹ!gyínáè	wóńgyínáè
ɔ̀agyìná	ɔ̀ágyíná	ɔ̀ǹgyínáè	ɔ́ńgyínáè
		(b) mèǹgyínáà	méńgyínáà
		wóǹ!gyínáà	wóńgyínáà
		ɔ̀ǹgyínáà	ɔ́ńgyínáà

180

5. Progressive

mèrègyìná	mérèngyìná
wóregyìná / wòregyìná (Fa)	wórèngyìná
ɔ̀règyìná	ɔ̀rèngyìná

6. Future I

mbɛ́!gyíná	méngyìná
wóbɛ́!gyíná / wòbɛ́!gyíná (Fa)	wóngyìná
ɔ̀bɛ́!gyíná	ɔ́ngyìná

7. Future II

Ak.As.	Fa.	Negative
mèrèbɛ̀gyìná	mèrèbɛ́!gyíná	(same as for Future I)
wórèbɛ̀gyìná	wòrèbɛ́!gyíná	
ɔ̀rèbɛ̀gyìná	ɔ̀rèbɛ́!gyíná	

8. Consecutive

	Ak.As.	Fa.	
(na)	màgyíná	màágyíná	màngyìná
	wóá!gyíná	wóágyíná	wóângyìnà /wòàngyìná (Fa)
	ɔ̀àgyíná	ɔ̀ágyíná	ɔ̀àngyìná

(**Negative** : see also **Note** on pages 175-176.

9. Imperative I (Simple)

gyìnà	ngyìná (Ak.As)
	m̀má ngyìná (Fa)

10. Imperative II (Optative)

(mà) méṅgyíná   (m̀má) méṅ̀ngyìná
   ɔ̀ṅgyíná   ɔ̀ṅ̀ngyìná

D   Disyllabic Tone Group III : bisa 'ask'

1. Habitual

Ak. As.	Fa.	Ak. As.	Fa.
mèbìsá	mèbísá / mèbísà	mèmbìsá	mèmbísà
wòbìsá	wòbísá / wòbísà	wòmbìsá	wòmbísà
ɔ̀bìsá	ɔ̀bísá / ɔ̀bísà	ɔ̀mbìsá	ɔ̀mbísà

2. Stative : not applicable

3. Past

(a) mèbìsáè   màmbìsá (Ak.As)   màmbísà (Fa)
   wòbìsáè / wòbìsáè (Fa)   wóámbìsá   wòàmbísà
   ɔ̀bìsáè   ɔ̀àmbìsá   ɔ̀àmbísà

(b) mèbìsáà
   wòbìsáà / wòbìsáà (Fa)
   ɔ̀bìsáà

4. Perfect

Ak. As.	Fa.		Ak. As.	Fa.
màbísá	màábísá / -bísà	(a) mèmbísáè	mémbísáè
wóá!bísá	wóábísá / - bísà	wóm!bísáè	wómbísáè
ɔ̀àbísá	ɔ̀àbísá / -bísá	ɔ̀mbísáè	ɔ̀mbísáè
		(b) mèmbísáà	mémbísáà
		wóm!bísáà	wómbísáà
		ɔ̀mbísáà	ɔ̀mbísáà

5. Progressive

Ak. As.	Fa.	Ak. As.	Fa.
mèrèbìsá	mèrèbísá /- bísà	mérémbìsá	mérémbísà
wórèbìsa	wòrèbísá /- bísà	wórémbìsa	wórémbísà
ɔrèbìsá	ɔrèbísá /- bísà	ɔrémbìsá	ɔrémbísà

6. Future I

Ak. As.	Fa.	Ak. As.	Fa
mbébí lsá	mbébísá / -bísà	mémbìsá	mémbísà
wóbébí lsá	wòbébísá / -bísà	wómbìsá	wómbísà
ɔbɛbí lsá	ɔbébísá / -bísà	ɔmbìsa	ɔmbìsà

7. Future II

Ak. As.	Fa.	Negative
mèrèbɛbí lsá	mèrèbébísá / -bísà	(same as for Future I)
wórèbɛbí lsá	wòrèbébísá / -bísà	
ɔrèbɛbí lsá	ɔrèbébísá / -bísà	

8. Consecutive

	Ak. As.	Fa.	Ak. As.	Fa
(na)	màbísá	màabísá / -bísà	màmbìsà	màmbìsa
	wóálbísá	wóábísá / -bísà	wóámbìsá	wòàmbísà
	ɔàbísá	ɔábísá / -bísà	ɔàmbìsá	ɔàmbísà

(Negative: see also **note** on pages 175-176)

9. Imperative I (Simple)

bìsà

mbìsá (Ak.As)

`mmá mbísà (Fa)

10. Imperative II (Optative)

	Fa.*	Ak.As.	Fa.
(mà) mémbísá	mémbísà	(m̀má) mèm̀mbìsá	mèm̀mbísà
ɔ́mbísá	ɔ́mbísà	ɔ̀m̀mbìsá	ɔ̀m̀mbísà

* Fante has two tone patterns in the affirmative.

II INGRESSIVE VERBS

The Ingressive prefixes are bɛ and kɔ which are used with 7 of the 10 Tense / Aspect forms of the verb to indicate a movement towards or away from the speaker that is required before the action indicated by the verb. These prefixes do not occur with the Stative and Future I and II forms of the verb.

In the following examples only forms with the prefix bɛ are given. The tone patterns are the same when the prefix kɔ is used.

A Monosyllabic Verb stem : da 'sleep'

1. Habitual

Ak. As.	Fa.	Ak. As.	Fa.
mèbɛ́dá	mèbɛ́dá / -dà	mèm̀bɛ́dá	mèm̀bɛ́dá / -dà
wóbɛ́dá	wòbɛ́dá / -dà	wóm̀bɛ́dá	wòm̀bɛ́dá / -dà
ɔ̀bɛ́dá	ɔ̀bɛ́dá / -dà	ɔ́m̀bɛ́dá	ɔ̀m̀bɛ́dá / -dà

2. Stative

Not applicable

3. Past

		Ak. As.	Fa.
mèbɛ̀dáè		màm̀bɛ̀dá	màm̀bɛ́dá
wóbɛ̀dáè / wòbɛ̀dáè (Fa)		wóàm̀bɛ̀dá	wòàm̀bɛ̀dá
ɔ̀bɛ̀dáè		ɔ̀àm̀bɛ̀dá	ɔ̀àm̀bɛ́dá

4. Perfect

Ak. As.	Fa.	Ak. As.	Fa.
màbɛ́dá	màábɛ́dá / -dà	mèmbɛ́dáè	mémbɛ́dáè
wóá!bɛ́dá	wóábɛ́dá / -dà	wóm!bɛ́dáè	wómbɛ́dáè
ɔ̀àbɛ̀dá	ɔ́àbɛ́dá / -dà	ɔ̀mbɛ́dáè	ɔ́mbɛ́dáè

5. Progressive

Ak. As.	Fa.	Ak. As.	Fa.
mèrèbɛ̀da	mèrèbɛ́dá	mérémbɛ̀dá	mérémbɛ́dá
wórèbɛ̀dá	wòrèbɛ́dá	wórémbɛ́dá	wórémbɛ́dá
ɔ̀rèbɛ̀dá	ɔ̀rèbɛ́dá	ɔ́rémbɛ̀dá	ɔ́rémbɛ́dá

6. Future I

Not applicable

7. Future II

Not applicable

8. Consecutive

Ak.As.	Fa.	Ak. As.	Fa.
(na) màbɛ́dá	mà`àbɛ́dá	(na) màmbɛ̀dá	màmbɛ́dá
wóá!bɛ́dá	wóábɛ́dá	wóámbɛ̀dá	wòàmbɛ́dá
ɔ̀àbɛ́dá	ɔ̀àbɛ́dá	ɔ̀àmbɛ̀dá	ɔ̀àmbɛ́dá

(**Negative**: see also note on pages 175-176)

9. Imperative I

Ak. As.	Fa.	Ak. As.	Fa.
bɛ̀dá	bɛ́dá	m̀bɛ̀dá	m̀má m̀bɛ́dá / -dà

10. Imperative II

		Ak. As.	Fa.
(mà) mémbɛ́dá		(m̀mà) mèm̀mbɛ̀dá	mèm̀mbɛ́dá
ɔ́mbɛ́dá		ɔ̀m̀mbɛ̀dá	ɔ̀m̀mbɛ́dá

B Disyllabic - Tone Group I stem : tɔn 'sell'

1. Habitual

Ak. As.	Fa.	Ak. As.	Fa.
mèbὲtɔ́ń	mèbétɔ́ń	mèmbὲtɔ́ń	mèmbétɔ́ń
wóbὲtɔ́ń	wòbétɔ́ń	wómbὲtɔ́ń	wòmbétɔ́ń
ɔ̀bὲtɔ́ń	ɔ̀bétɔ́ń	ɔ̀mbὲtɔ́ń	ɔ̀mbétɔ́ń

2. Stative

Not applicable

3. Past

	Ak. As.	Fa.
mèbὲtɔ́nèè		màmbὲtɔ́ń	màmbétɔ́ń
wóbὲtɔ́nèè / wòbὲtɔ́nèè (Fa)		wóàmbὲtɔ́ń	wòàmbétɔ́ń
ɔ̀bὲtɔ́nèè		ɔ̀àmbὲtɔ́ń	ɔ̀àmbétɔ́ń

4. Perfect

Ak. As.	Fa.	Ak.As.	Fa.
màbétɔ́ń	màabétɔ́ń	mèmbétɔ́nèè	mémbétɔ́nèè
wóàlbétɔ́ń	wóábétɔ́ń	wómlbétɔ́nèè	wómbétɔ́nèè
ɔ̀àbétɔ́ń	ɔ̀ábétɔ́ń	ɔ̀mbétɔ́nèè	ɔ́mbétɔ́nèè

5. Progressive

Ak.As.	Fa.	Ak.As.	Fa.
mèrèbὲtɔ́ń	mèrèbétɔ́ń	mérémbὲtɔ́ń	mérémbétɔ́ń
wórèbὲtɔ́ŕ	wòrèbétɔ́ń	wórémbὲtɔ́ń	wórémbétɔ́ń
ɔ̀rèbὲtɔ́ń	ɔ̀rèbétɔ́ń	ɔ́rémbὲtɔ́ń	ɔ́rémbétɔ́ń

6. Future I

Not applicable

7. **Future II**   Not applicable

8. **Consective**

Ak. As.	Fa.	Ak. As.	Fa.
(na) màbétɔ́ń	màabétɔ́ń	(na) màm̀bὲtɔ́ń	màm̀bétɔ́ń
wóálbétɔ́ń	wóábétɔ́ń	wóám̀bὲtɔ́ń	wòàm̀bétɔ́ń
ɔ̀abétɔ́ń	ɔ̀ábétɔ́ń	ɔ̀àm̀bὲtɔ́ń	ɔ̀àm̀bétɔ́ń

9. **Imperative I**

Ak. As.	Fa.	Ak. As.	Fa.
bὲtɔ́ń	bétɔ́ń	m̀bὲtɔ́ń	m̀má m̀bétɔ́ń

10. **Imperative II**

		Ak. As.	Fa.
mà mém̀bétɔ́ń	m̀má	mèm̀m̀bétɔ́ń	mèm̀m̀bétɔ́ń
ɔm̀bétɔ́ń		ɔ̀m̀m̀bétɔ́ń	ɔ̀m̀m̀bétɔ́ń

C   Disyllabic - Tone Group II stem : gyina   'stand / stop'

1. **Habitual**

Ak. As.	Fa.	Ak. As.	Fa.
mèbὲgyìná	mèbél̩gyíná	mèm̀bὲgyìná	mèm̀bél̩gyíná
wóbὲgyìná	wòbél̩gyíná	wóm̀bὲgyìná	wòm̀bél̩gyíná
ɔ̀bὲgyìná	ɔ̀bél̩gyíná	ɔ̀m̀bὲgyìná	ɔ̀m̀bél̩gyíná

2. **Stative**   Not applicable

3. **Past**

Ak. As.	Fa.	Ak. As.	Fa.
mèbὲgyìnàè	mèbὲgyínàè	màm̀bὲgyìná	màm̀bél̩gyíná
wóbὲgyìnàè	wòbὲgyínàè	wóám̀bὲgyìná	wòàm̀bél̩gyíná
ɔ̀bὲgyìnàè	ɔ̀bὲgyínàè	ɔ̀m̀bὲgyìná	ɔ̀àm̀bél̩gyíná

4. Perfect

Ak. As.	Fa.	Ak. As.	Fa.
màbɛ́!gyíná	màabɛ́!gyíná	mèmbɛ́!gyínàè	mémbɛ́!gyínàè
wóà!bɛ́!gyíná	wóabɛ́!gyíná	wómbɛ́!gyínàè	wómbɛ́!gyínàè
ɔ̀àbɛ́!gyíná	ɔ̀àbɛ́!gyíná	ɔ̀mbɛ́!gyínàè	ɔ́mbɛ́!gyínàè

5. Progressive

Ak. As.	Fa.	Ak. As.	Fa.
mèrebɛgyìná	mèrebɛ́!gyíná	mérémbɛgyìná	mèrémbɛ́!gyíná
wórebɛgyìná	wòrebɛ́!gyíná	wórémbɛgyìná	wòrémbɛ́!gyíná
ɔ̀rebɛgyìná	ɔ̀rebɛ́!gyíná	ɔ́rémbɛgyìná	ɔ̀rémbɛ́!gyíná

6. Future I Not applicable

7. Future II Not applicable

8. Consecutive

Ak. As.	Fa.	Ak. As.	Fa.
(na) màbɛ́!gyíná	màabɛ́!gyíná	(na) màmbɛgyìná	màmbɛ́!gyíná
wóà!bɛ́!gyíná	wóabɛ́!gyíná	wóámbɛgyìná	wòambɛ́!gyíná
ɔ̀àbɛ́!gyíná	ɔ̀àbɛ́!gyíná	ɔ̀àmbɛgyìná	ɔ̀àmbɛ́!gyíná

(**Negative:** see also note on pages 175-176)

9. Imperative I

bɛgyìná

mbɛgyìná (Ak. As)

m̀má mbɛ́!gyíná (Fa)

10. Imperative II

	Ak. As.	Fa.
(mà) mémbɛ́!gyíná	(mmá) mèmmbɛgyìná	mèmmbɛ́!gyíná
ɔ́mbɛ́!gyíná	ɔ̀mmbɛgyìná	ɔ̀mmbɛ́!gyíná

188

D **Disyllabic - Tone Group III stem** : bisa 'ask'

1. Habitual

Ak. As.	Fa.	Ak. As.	Fa.
mèbèbísá	mèbébísà / -bísá	mèmbèbí !sá	mèmbébísà
wóbèbísá	wòbébísà / -bísá	wómbèbí !sá	wòmbébísà
ɔbèbísá	ɔbébísà / -bísá	ɔmbèbí !sá	ɔmbébísà

2. Stative Not applicable

3. Past

Ak.	Fa.	As.	Ak. As.	Fa.
mèbèbísáè	mèbèbìsáè	mèbèbísàè	màmbèbí !sá	màmbébísà
wóbèbísáè	wóbèbìsáè	wóbèbísàè	wóámbèbí !sá	wòàmbébísà
ɔbèbísáè	ɔbèbìsáè	ɔbèbísàè	ɔàmbèbí !sá	ɔàmbébísà

4. Perfect

Ak. As.	Fa.	Ak.	Fa.	As.
màbébí !sá	màábébísà	mèmbébísáè	mémbébísáè	mèmbébísàè
wóá!bébí !sá	wóábébísà	wòmbébísáè	wómbébísáè	wòmbébísàè
ɔàbébí !sá	ɔábébísà	ɔmbébísáè	ɔmbébísáè	ɔmbébísàè

5. Progressive

Ak. As.	Fa.	Ak. As.	Fa.
mèrébèbí !sá	mèrèbé / -bísà	mérémbèbí !sá	mèrémbébísà
wórébèbí !sá	wòrèbébísá / -bísà	wórémbèbí !sá	wòrémbébísà
ɔrébèbí !sá	ɔrèbébísá / -bísà	ɔrémbèbí !sá	ɔrémbébísà

6. Future I Not applicable

7. Future II Not applicable

8. Consecutive

Ak. As.	Fa.		Ak. As.	Fa.
(na) màbébí lsá	màábέbísá/-bísà	(na)	màṁbέbí lsá	màṁbέbísà
wóálbέbí lsá	wóábέbísá/-bísà		wóáṁbέbí lsá	wòàṁbέbísà
ɔ̀abέbí lsá	ɔ̀ábέbísá/-bísà		ɔ̀aṁbέbí lsá	ɔ̀aṁbέbísà

(See also **Note** on pages 175-176.)

9. Imperative I

Ak. As.	Fa.	Ak. As.	Fa.
bὲbí lsá	bεbísá/-bísà	ṁbεbí lsà	ṁmá ṁbεbísà

10. Imperative II

Ak. As.	Fa.	Ak. As.	Fa.
(mà) mémbέbí lsá	mémbέbísà	(ṁmà) mèṁṁbέbí lsá	mèṁṁbέbísà
ɔ́mbέbí lsá	ɔ́mbέbísà	ɔ̀ṁmbέbí lsá	ɔ̀ṁṁbέbísà

SPECIMEN PASSAGES IN AKAN

The following are two specimen passages. Each is first presented in the orthographies of the three written dialects - Akuapem, Fante and Asante - and then in the unified Akan orthography.

The reproduction of these passages in this book has been made possible by the kind permission of the Bureau of Ghana Languages, Accra.

PASSAGE 1

Asante

Kookoo nkɔsoɔ no firi adinkanfoɔ no, asase pa, ɔmannwoeɛ ne adwadie ne emu sikapɛ ne sikanibereɛ ne adepɛ deɛ, nanso ɛfiri ɔmanfoɔ no ankasa mmɔdenbɔ nso. Wɔammɔ wɔn ho mmɔden amfa aniɛden anyɔ a, anka ansi baabiara. Aman bi so deɛ, nnipa mfuamfua a wɔyɛ adefoɔ no ɛwɔ kookoo akɛseakɛse a nnipa yɔ mu adwuma. Nanso yɛn ha deɛ, akuafoɔ dɔɔso a obiara yɛ ne deɛ fa.

Akuapem

Kookoo nkɔso no fi adikanfo, asase pa, ɔmannwoe ne aguadi ne mu sikapɛ ne sika nibere ne adepɛ de, nanso efi ɔmanfo no ankasa mmɔdenbɔ nso. Wɔammɔ wɔn ho mmɔden amfa anuɔden anyɛ a, anka ansi baabiara. Aman bi so de, nnipa mmaako-mmaaako a wɔyɛ adefo na ɛwɔ kookoo akɛseakɛse a nnipa yɛ mu adwuma. Nanso yɛn ha de, akuafo dɔɔso a obiara yɛ ne de fa.

Fante

Kookoo nkɔdo no fi edzikanfo no, asaase pa, amandwee na eguadzi na no mu sikapɛ, na sikaenyiber na adzepɛ dze, naaso of ɔmanfo no ankasa mbɔdzembɔ so. Wɔammbɔ hɔn ho mbɔdzen ammfa anyiɔdzen annyɛ a, nkyɛ ennkesi hwee. Aman bi do dze, nyimpa nkornkor a wɔyɛ adzefo nna wɔwɔ kookoo akɛseakɛse a nkrɔfo yɛ mu edwuma. Naaso hɛn ha dze ekuafo dɔɔso a obiara yɛ ne dze fa.

AKAN

Kookoo nkɔso no fi adikanfo no, asaase pa, ɔmandwoe ne aguadi ne ɛmu sikapɛ, ne sikaanbere ne adepɛ de, nanso ɛfi ɔmanfo no ankasa mbɔdenbɔ nso. Wɔambɔ wɔn ho mbɔden amfa aniɛden anyɛ a, anka ankosi hwee. Aman bi so de, nnipa mfuamfua a wɔyɛ adefo na wɔwɔ kookoo akɛseakɛse a nkurɔfo yɛ mu adwuma. Nanso yɛn ha de, akuafo dɔɔso a obiara yɛ ne de fa.

PASSAGE 2

Fante

Hɔ nyinara taa dzinn, osiandɛ nna Nana nntum mpata n'enyiwa. Afei nna ne meneba esiw ma onntum nnkasa bio. Ɔhyɛɛ ne kasaa ase bio no ɔfrɛɛ edumfo hɔn panyin no dɛ ɔmfa daduanyi no mbra. Ɔrekasa nyinara nna Kofi da dan mu, ntsi nna obiara nnyae nnhun nyia oedzi dɛm ewu no. Wɔdze no puei ara

192

na adze bɔɔ ne maame do. Nna hɔ ayɛ huhuhuhu dɛmara.
Kyerɛkyerɛnyi a obiara dzi no nyi wɔ Ayɛtse hɔ no nna oekedzi
ewu a ɔtse dɛm yi? Nna obiara nngye ndzi dɛ obotum ayɛ adze a
ɔtse dɛm.

Akuapem

Ɛhɔ nyinaa tɛm dinn, esiane sɛ na Nana ntumi mpata n'ani.
Afei na ne menewa asiw ma ontumi nkasa bio. Ofii ne kasa ase
bio no, ɔtɾɛɛ adumfo payin no sɛ ɔmfa deduani no mmra.
ɔrekasa nyinaa na Kofi da dan mu enti na obiara nnya nhuu nea
wadi saa awu no. Wɔde no puei ara na ade tɔɔ ne maame so. Na
ɛhɔ ayɛ huhuhuhu saa ara. Ɔkyerɛkyerɛfo a obiara di no ni wɔ
Ayɛte hɔ no na wakɔdi awu a ɛte sɛ yi? Na obiara nnye nni sɛ
obetumi ayɛ ade a ɛte saa.

Asante

Ɛhɔ nyinaa taa dinn, ɛsiane sɛ na Nana ntumi mpata n'ani.
Afei na ne menewa asi ma ɔntumi nkasa bio. Ɔhyɛɛ ne kasa ase
bio no, ɔfɾɛɛ adumfoɔ panin no sɛ ɔmfa deduani no mmra.
ɔrekasa nyinaa na Kofi da dan mu. Enti na obiara nya nhunuu
deɛ wadi saa awu no. Wɔde no pueiɛ ara na adeɛ tɔɔ ne maame
so. Na ɛhɔ ayɛ huhuhuhu saa ara. Kyerɛkyerɛfoɔ a obiara di no
ni wɔ Ayɛte hɔ no na wakɔdi awu a ɛte saa yi? Na obiara nnye
nni sɛ obetumi ayɛ adeɛ a ɛte saa.

193

Ɛhɔ nyinaa taa dinn, ɛsiane sɛ na Nana ntumi mpata n'aniwa.
Afei na ne menewa asiw ma ɔntumi nkasa bio. Ɔhyɛɛ ne kasa
ase bio no ɔfrɛɛ adumfo wɔn panyin no sɛ ɔmfa daduani no
mbra. Ɔrekasa nyinaa na Kofi da dan mu nti na obiara nnya nhuu
nea ɔadi saa awu no. Wɔde no puei ara na ade tɔɔ ne maame so.
Na ɛhɔ ayɛ huhuhuhu saa ara. Ɔkyerɛkyerɛni a obiara di no ni
wɔ Ayɛte hɔ no na ɔakɔdi awu a ɛte saa yi? Na obiara ngye ndi
sɛ ɔbɛtumi ayɛ ade a ɛte saa.

Map.1 GHANA : THE DISTRIBUTION OF THE AKAN (TWI FANTE) LANGUAGE AND ITS DIALECTS

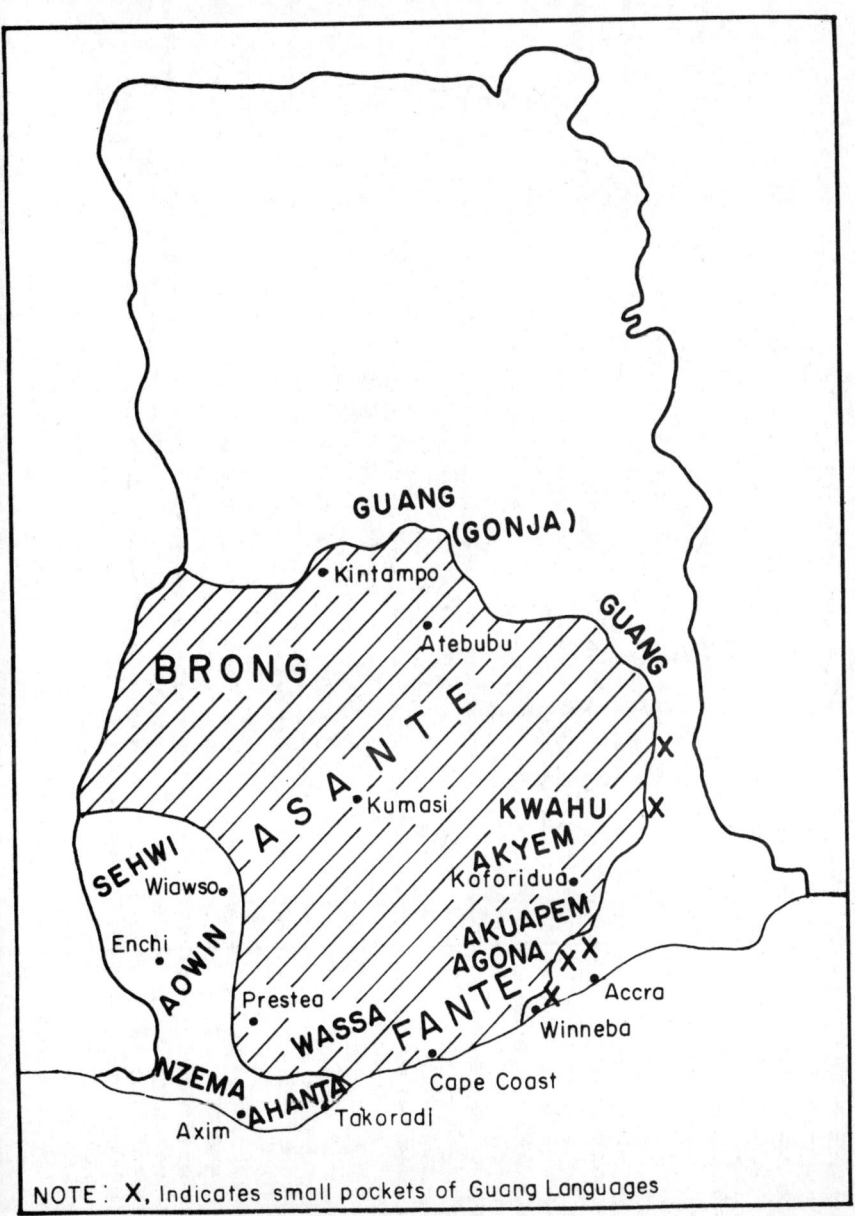

NOTE : **X**, Indicates small pockets of Guang Languages

Map 2. GHANA: PART OF LA COTE D'IVOIRE AND
AND TOGO SHOWING THE DISTRIBUTION OF THE
TANO LANGUAGE SPOKEN BY THE AKAN
ETHNIC GROUP

A

Adjectives
  in compounds, 122, 124.
  reduplication of, 135-136,
  137-138.
  tone of, 78.
Advanced tongue root
  consonants, 21, 34, 43-44, 45.
Advanced tongue root harmony,
  14-17.
Adverbs, tone of, 78.
Affixes, 80, 82.
  adjectival, 86-87.
  nominal, 82-86.
  verbal, 87-97.
Akan
  dialects, vii-viii.
  speakers, vii.
  specimen texts in, 192, 194.
  unified orthography, 154-167.
Akuapem
  labialisation in, 145-146.
  nasalised vowels in, 4.
  rounding of vowels in, 147.
  specimen texts in, 191, 193.
Alveolar consonants, 26.
  palatalisation of, 144.
Alveolo-palatal consonants, 26.
Asante
  labialisation in, 145-146.
  nominal suffix in, 83-84, 85-86,
  149, 159.
  palatalisation in, 144-145.
  rounding of vowels in, 146-147.
  specimen texts in, 191, 193
  vowel alternation in, 147-148.
Aspect affixes, 92-96, 155-156.

Assimilation
  homorganic nasal, 142-143.
  vowel harmony, 24.

C

Compounds, 80, 117-138.
  phonology of, 117-136.
  tone of nouns in, 74-75.
  vowel harmony in, 24-25, 156.
Consecutive verb, 93, 175-176.
  negative of, 175-176.
Consonants, 26-51.
  representation of, 161-163.
  syllabic, 53.

D

Dialects of Akan, vii.
Disyllabic stems, 100-110.
  reduplication of, 127-131.
  tone of, 113-116.
Downdrift, 56-58.
Downstepped High tone
  automatic, 56-57.
  non-automatic, 58-59.
  derived, 59-60.
  lexical, 59.

F

Falling pitch, 61-65.
Fante
  labialisation in, 145-146.
  nasalised vowels in, 4.
  palatalisation in, 144.

Fante (contd.)
  rounding of vowels in,146-147.
  specimen texts, 192.
Future verb, 92, 156-157,
  174-175, 179, 181, 183.

G

Glottal consonants, 27
  glottal stop, 48-51.
Gold Coast script
  vowels in, 17-18.
Grammatical tone, 66-74.

H

Habitual verb, 67-68, 173, 177,
  180, 182, 184, 186, 187, 189.
High tone, 55-56.
  stem, 111.
High vowels, 6,7, 8,147.
Homorganic nasal assimilation,
  142-143.

I

Imperative verbs, 176-177, 179,
  181-182, 183-184, 185, 187,
  188, 190.
Ingressive
  prefixes, 16, 95, 156.
  verbs, 184-190.

K

Kinship nouns, 72, 85.

L

Labial consonants
  palatalisation of, 144.
Labialisation, 28, 145-146.

Labial-palatalisation, 28.
Lexical tone, 66.
Low tone, 56.
  stem, 111-112.
Low vowel, 6, 7.

M

Mid tone, 55, 58.
Mid vowels, 6,7.
  nasality in, 4.
Monosyllabic stems, 98-99,
  nasality in, 98-100.
  reduplication of, 125-127.
  tone of, 111-112.

N

Nasal consonants, 27, 29, 38-42.
  homorganic, 95-97, 118.
Nasalisation
  in CV stems, 98-99.
  of consonants, 120, 141-142,
  161-162.
Negative prefix, 96-97, 157.
Nouns
  alienable, 71.
  Asante noun suffix, 11-12,
  83-84.
  inalienable, 71.
  in compounds, 120-124.
  reduplicated, 136, 138.
  tone of, 69-78.

O

Orthography
  unified Akan, 154-167.

P

Palatal consonant, 27, 29.
  in vowel harmony, 20-21.

Palatalisation, 28, 143-145, 161.
Past Tense, 10-11, 143-145.
  suffix, 93-95, 156, 158.
Perfect prefix, 93.
Possessive noun phrase
  tone of, 69-74.
Possessive pronouns, 19, 156,
  158-159.
Prefixes
  adjectival, 86.
  nominal, 82-83.
  pronoun, 15, 87-91.
  verbal, 87-93.
Progressive verb, 11, 111, 174,
  178, 181, 183, 185, 186, 188.
  189.
Pronouns, 87-91.
  representation of, 158-159.

R

Reduplication,
  of adjective, 135-136.
  of noun, 136, 138.
  of verb, 125-135.
  vowel harmony in, 18, 19.
Rounding harmony, 16-17.
  rounding of vowels, 146-147.

S

Stative verb, 67, 112, 173, 177,
  180.
Stems
  disyllabic, 100-110, 113-116.
  monosyllabic, 81, 97-100,
  111-113.
  other, 110.

Subordinate verb
  tone of, 69.
Subject-concord prefixes, 87-91.
Suffix
  adjectival, 86-87.
  nominal, 11-12, 83-86,
  verbal, 93-95.
Syllable, 52-54.

T

Tense
  tense/apsect affixes, 92-96,
  140, 153.
Tone
  complex, 62-64.
  downstepped high, 59-61.
  grammatical, 66-75.
  high, 55-56.
  lexical, 66.
  low, 56.
  of adjectives, 78.
  of adverbs, 78.
  of nouns, 69-75, 76-78.
  of verbs, 75-76, 111-116.

V

Velar consonant, 27, 29.
Vowel
  chart, 7.
  description of, 5-7.
  distribution of, 7-14.
  harmony, 14-25, 139-140,
  154-156.